$\dfrac{12.-}{\in}$

$\left(4 - 17^{00} \right)$
Hist - E. Europe

Comrade and Lover

Rosa Luxemburg's Letters to Leo Jogiches

Comrade and Lover
Rosa Luxemburg's Letters to Leo Jogiches

Edited and translated by Elżbieta Ettinger

The MIT Press
Cambridge, Massachusetts, and London, England

Translated material in this volume was selected from the original Polish edition, *Róża Luksemburg: Listy do Leona Jogichesa-Tyszki* (Ksiazka i Wiedza, 1968-1971).

Photographs courtesy of
Centralne Archiwum KC P2PR,
Warsaw, Poland.

This book was set in Palatino and Optima by DEKR Corporation, and printed and bound by The Murray Printing Company in the United States of America

Library of Congress Cataloging in Publication Data

Luxemburg, Rosa, 1870-1919.
  Comrade and lover.

  Selected letters originally published under title: Róża Luksemburg: Listy do Leona Jogichesa-Tyszki.
  Bibliography: p.
  Includes index.
  1. Communists—Correspondence. 2. Communists—Biography. 3. Jogiches, Leo, 1867-1917. 4. Luxemburg Rosa, 1870-1919. I. Jogiches, Leo, 1867-1919. II. Ettinger, Elżbieta. III. Title.
HX276.L8433   1979   335.43'092'4 [B]   79-9327
ISBN 0-262-05021-8

Contents

Editor's Note   *viii*

Introduction   *xiii*

The Letters

The First Years: 1893–1897   1
The Trial: 1898–1900   27
Together: 1900–1906   109
Unto Death . . .: 1907–1914   161

Epilogue   *189*

Appendix: Historical Note   *195*

List of Letters   *197*

Index   *201*

To Maia

Editor's Note

Rosa Luxemburg wrote nearly a thousand letters to Leo Jogiches, her lover and comrade. The letters were published in the original Polish in three volumes (Róża Luksemburg, *Listy do Leona Jogichesa-Tyszki, 1893-1914,* Warsaw: Książka i Wiedza, 1968-1971), expertly edited and annotated by Professor Feliks Tych. Professor Tych subsequently found and, in 1976, published some additional letters, two of which are included in this selection.

Luxemburg was a prolific letter writer. She corresponded with her parents in Warsaw and with each of her four siblings, with friends and comrades, and with socialists all over Europe. Almost all her letters are now available and many have been translated into English. However, this is the first English translation of her letters to Jogiches.

In preparing this volume, I had several options: publishing all the letters; selecting letters dealing with Luxemburg's involvement with the Socialist International, the Social Democracy of the Kingdom of Poland and Lithuania (SDKPiL), the Polish Socialist Party (PPS), and the German Social Democratic Party (SPD); or concentrating on her personal relationship with Jogiches. While the first two would have provided students of the European, and especially the Polish, Russian, and German socialist movements, with a wealth of material, they would have left Luxemburg as she is at present—faceless.

The third choice would reveal a woman, hitherto unknown, whose sex did not diminish her political stature and whose politics did not interfere with her private life. It would also expose the fragility of the concept that a woman cannot, without giving up love, realize her talent.

Annotations presented another dilemma. Fortunately I was reminded by Elena Wilson of her husband Edmund's remark about a work "knee-deep or waist-deep or neck-deep in huge footnotes." I have kept them to a bare minimum. The only time when Luxemburg allowed herself to be herself was in her letters to Jogiches. To let their spontaneity be diminished by the weight of footnotes would have defeated my purpose.

And finally the translation. If "traduttore-traditore" is true, it is peculiarly true for love letters written in Polish and rendered into English. That love has an international language must be sadly denied by every translator. The Polish language of love with its wealth of tender, intimate words, and the possibility of creating words, inimitable words, private, yet understandable to an outsider, cannot be adequately translated into English due to the differences in cultures and in the morphology of the two languages.

In her letters to Jogiches, Luxemburg does not write, she speaks to him. Sometimes it is a monologue, sometimes a dialogue, that she carries on with herself or with him. This sets the letters apart from those she wrote others. The latter are fine specimens of epistolary art. Moving and witty, sharp and businesslike, their tone is modulated according to the recipient. This is not true of her letters to Jogiches. Technically she follows the pattern of spoken rather than written language; emotionally she knows no patterns, no inhibitions (even if she claims she does), no restraints (except for letters she wrote after she broke with him—then every word is carefully weighed and weighted).

Luxemburg was a woman of impatient temper and great passion. This is reflected in the tone of the letters more than in the words, in the rhythm more than in the language. It is the tone and the emotional cadence that I have attempted to preserve, even if it meant deviating from a merely "correct" translation of the text. I felt I should not be more "correct" than the author lest I risk losing what is most gripping in the letters—authenticity.

I took liberties when a literal translation would have contradicted her spirit. Sometimes I translated the same Polish word in different ways, not to make her language richer but to get closer to her truth; her "dear" may well be also "my dear," or "my love," or "my dear one," depending on her mood and on the mood of the letter. Lexically and etymologically the English "dear" and the Polish *drogi* are identical, yet contextually, and especially conventionally, there is a vast difference between them.

The letters are often a continuation of Luxemburg-Jogiches conversations. They pick up where a conversation left off, and, as in a conversation, Luxemburg often jumps chaotically from one subject to another, leaves a thought hanging, a phrase disturbingly ambiguous. Whether it was ambiguous to Jogiches we will never know. Sometimes he demanded clarification, but given his idiosyncrasies, it did not necessarily mean that he could not follow her. Be that as it may, it would be presumptuous for me to "fill in" where she did not, to substitute an explication for a shortcut. Naturally the letters were not meant for publication. It would have offended Luxemburg to see them published; it would have angered her to see them "elaborated."

Another problem was posed by Luxemburg's mingling of different languages with Polish. She spoke German, Russian, and French, and was familiar with Yiddish, English, Italian, and Latin; her letters at times resemble a Gobelin tapestry. She mingled the languages out of haste, sometimes throwing in an incorrect foreign word (an additional problem), at others quoting an entire conversation in another tongue. With some exceptions, I decided to sacrifice this multilingual flavor for the sake of clarity and fluency. An inordinate number of footnotes and constant interruptions in the text did not seem to me a good substitute for the pungency of her letters.

The letters, numbered by me, are arranged in four sections in chronological order, with occasional rearrangement for thematic continuity. Each section is preceded by a biographical note. The dates of the letters, mostly missing, were determined by Professor Tych, the Polish editor, after long and meticulous research. A number of my footnotes are based on his findings. Any editorial deletion is indicated by ellipses in brackets: [. . .].

I would like to acknowledge the assistance of Krystyna Pomorska, Ilona Karmel, Mieczysław Maneli, Aileen Ward, J. L. Talmon, Myra Brenner, and Bert Hartry. My special thanks go to Diana H. Green and Feliks Tych. The MIT Old Dominion Fellowship made the completion of the book possible.

No couple on earth has the chance we have. . . .
We will both work and our life will be perfect. . . .
We will be happy, we must.

Rosa Luxemburg to Leo Jogiches
March 6, 1899

Introduction

1

Love and work, a union of minds and souls, was what Rosa Luxemburg dreamed of and struggled for during the fifteen years of her tempestuous affair with Leo Jogiches. They belonged together, not because they willed it but because they could not unwill it. Their happy times together were bliss. Their battles were bloody. They parted, loving each other, defeated.

From the beginning the relationship carried within itself the seeds of its own destruction. They were infected with the same fever—independence and individuality—which was the carrier of their ultimate failure. The common cause, socialism, which welded their lives together, failed to sustain Luxemburg's dream of a perfect union because each denied the other the freedom they both desired for mankind. They were drawn to socialism by the urge to remodel the world. Extended to their personal relationship, this urge was fatal. Luxemburg projected her ideal of a perfect international union of workers onto her union with Jogiches, and neither stood the test of life. Blind to the complexities of human nature, she was determined to make both Jogiches and mankind happy, but on her own terms.

Compromise and tolerance she did not know. Nor did Jogiches. Yet neither tired of inducing or seducing a concession from the other, perhaps to prove love, perhaps power. Surrender meant for each different things at different times, as did rebellion. Surrender could be equated with love, as rebellion with its lack, but it could also be a chance to dominate by provoking guilt. Each made claims on the other's independence, though its preservation was crucial for both. They never achieved the delicate balance between granting and restraining freedom. They depended on each other intellectually and emotionally, but unable to regard this dependence as a condition of love, they were resentful of the restrictions it imposed. They struggled constantly within themselves to give to each other the space to breathe, but they meted it out guardedly and jealously.

Luxemburg's letters (Jogiches's letters to her have not survived) mirror the various and overlapping stages of the struggle: the master/disciple, adored/adoring, and child/parent relationships, and the reverse of each. The man who considered himself her creator is addressed as "my child" or "Dyodyo" or "Chuchya," the first a pet name reserved for small boys, the other, for baby girls. If "Dyodyo" misbehaved, she would deny him the endearment. Back in her favor, his anger still seething, he in turn would answer coldly. The letters disclose their weapons: love, seduction, provocation, rewards, and punishments, and their underlying erotic currents. Both partners used the letters as a substitute for an everyday life together and as a means of controlling the other: "My decision to stop writing," Luxemburg informed Jogiches, "is not the act of vengeance you think it is. It is not a boycott either." The letters also served as a workshop in which political strategies were worked out, alliances negotiated, opposition forces gauged, ammunition—articles and speeches—jointly produced. And they show that in politics it is impossible to say where Luxemburg started and Jogiches ended.

Jogiches lived for his political work. He was a man with a mission to which everything, including Luxemburg, was subordinated. Even though she was not his first love, he needed the knowledge that he was *her* only love. Even if her joy clashed with his gloom, and her exuberance with his reticence, he could come out of his shell to ask her, "Do you love me? Passionately? Do you know there is a man named Dyodyo who belongs to you?"

To be the most important person in his life did not satisfy Luxemburg. Herself capable of both love and work, she saw no need to give up one for the sake of the other. She regarded his single-mindedness as a symptom of a disease that she alone could cure by "the might of love." She refused to reconcile herself to the concept of a revolutionary's life that the Russian anarchists Bakunin and Nechaev defined in the *Revolutionary Catechism*: "The revolutionary is a lost man; he has no interests of his own, no cause of his own; no feelings, no habits, no belongings; he does not even have a name. Everything in him is absorbed by a single, exclusive interest, a single thought, a single passion—the revolution. . . . All the tender feelings of family life, of friendship, love, gratitude, and even honor must be stifled in him by a single cold passion—the revolutionary cause." [1] Though Jogiches did not follow this dictum to the letter, it still was close to his ideal and to his needs.

Unwilling to accept the primacy of his choice, Luxemburg never stopped competing with her only rival—mankind. "Your letters contain *nothing but nothing* except for *The Workers' Cause*," she reproached him early in their relationship. This remained a recurring complaint. "When I open your letters and see six sheets covered with debates about the Polish Socialist Party," she wrote when their affair was ten years old, "and not a single word about . . . ordinary life, I feel faint."

"Constructive work" and "positive action," not renuncia-
tion of a home, a child, and worldly goods, were her tools
for remedying existing ills. She did not seek redemption in
thwarting her natural instincts, nor did she try to alleviate
the suffering of others by self-inflicted wounds. Not only
was asceticism alien to her nature, she also saw it as destruc-
tive. Personal happiness, which Jogiches considered an almost sinful waste, she viewed as a natural extension of her
fight for the right to happiness and fulfillment for all. "Despite everything you've told me," she wrote him, ". . . I keep
harping on the worn-out tune, making claims on personal
happiness. Yes, I do have an accursed longing for happiness
and am ready to haggle for my daily portion with the stubbornness of a mule."

It was probably partly their different backgrounds and
partly their natural dispositions that bred the conflicting concepts. Jogiches's rebellion against a "bourgeois" life—home,
family, possessions—started when he was in his teens. Born
into a prominent, wealthy, Jewish family, he renounced his
milieu. He exchanged his own family for the family of workers, and the gymnasium (high school) for a locksmith shop.
Terror as a weapon fascinated him, as did cloak-and-dagger
operations. Disliked for his despotic and arrogant manner,
he was respected as a conspirator of unique skills. By the
time he was twenty, he was in the forefront of the revolutionary movement in his native Wilno.

Luxemburg came from a family of modest means. If she
did not know poverty, she did see her father struggling to
make ends meet. Her childhood was affected by a wrongly
diagnosed hip disease that left her with a bad limp. The
closely knit family doted on her, the youngest child, and she
grew into a self-confident girl. She was educated at a financial sacrifice and, though already deeply involved in the revolutionary movement in her teens, she graduated from the
Warsaw gymnasium at the top of her class. She learned early

that although knowledge was indispensable to carry on the struggle, life could not be lived fully without love, family, and friends.

Both Luxemburg and Jogiches, faced with prison, had to flee the czarist police. For Jogiches exile was the end of power; for Luxemburg, it was the beginning.

Exile came to Jogiches as a shock from which he never fully recovered. In Wilno, his life had been in constant danger, which set him apart from the detested bourgeoisie. In Switzerland there was no danger to make the revolutionary's life worth living. Instead there was the tranquillity of the university, for which he had as little use as he had formerly had for the gymnasium, and there were the trappings of the middle-class life he now led. He lived on the very family wealth he condemned, and this set him apart from his impecunious fellow exiles. Marxist theorists replaced the company of workers; inactivity, the daredevil deeds. His bent for force and command was little appreciated in theoretical disputes. Soon he found himself isolated. His past exploits had left him convinced of his superior mind, but cut off from his native soil, his work, and from the mother he worshipped, he, in Luxemburg's words, "vegetated in constant bitterness." Fear of failing beset him and never let him go.

Luxemburg, thrown back on her inner resources in an alien land, did not feel threatened. She remained attached to her family and to her country without the feeling of permanent loss that never left Jogiches. The different cultures, Jewish, Polish, German, and Russian, that she had absorbed in childhood made adaptation easier for her. If anything, she saw a better chance to "run and run after justice" in Switzerland than in the shadow of the Russian gallows. She attended the Zurich University as dutifully as she had previously attended the gymnasium, challenged the Swiss professors with her unconventional Marxist education, and ended her studies with a highly acclaimed doctoral dissertation. Jogiches left the university after ten years without obtaining a degree.

They met in Zurich in 1890 when Jogiches was twenty-three and Luxemburg was twenty. Though not a beauty, she fascinated men with her womanliness, her strength, and her brilliant mind. If her disproportionately large upper body and short child-like legs, a result of her childhood hip disease, marred her looks, self-deprecating irony added to her charm. Lustrous dark eyes beneath masses of rich brown hair and her passionate nature mesmerized men and women alike. She fell in love with Jogiches immediately; his burning inspiration and his aloofness made him seem a Dostoevskian hero. Time never changed that first impression. Throughout her life he remained the only man able to challenge her intellectually and tantalize her sexually. He found in her an intellect and a woman, both hungry; that he could nourish both gave him pleasure and a sense of power.

To say that only the "common cause" held them together would be an understatement. To say that mutual attraction held them together would be inaccurate. It is doubtful they could have been attracted to each other for more than a fleeting moment had they not been attracted to socialism as well. Together, in 1893, they founded the first significant Polish Marxist workers' party, the Social Democracy of the Kingdom of Poland. After evolutions and revolutions, it is still recognized as the forerunner of the ruling party in contemporary Poland.

If the small party into which Luxemburg had drawn Jogiches to entice him out of his growing isolation was a far cry from his own grandiose designs, it started Luxemburg on a career that placed her among the leaders of socialism in Europe. It was Jogiches who fathered her success; he provided the skills and the money. Above all, he recognized in her a genius which could reach its true heights, he felt, only under his tutelage. Indeed, she herself was rather skeptical at first about her possibilities. After meeting the father of Russian Marxism, Georgii V. Plekhanov, she wrote to a friend, "I was in Mornex but won't go there anymore because Plekhanov is too sophisticated or, to be exact, too well-educated for me. What could he possibly gain from a conversation with me? He knows everything better than I do, and I cannot create 'ideas'—original, genuine ideas." [2] A year later Jogiches's able, if only, disciple challenged Plekhanov's authority. Yet she often turned to Jogiches for "ideas"—"just give me a few ideas . . . *writing* is no problem for me." Before long the two had achieved the kind of near-perfect cooperation attainable when two minds become one. Intellectually they breathed in rhythm, a sort of cerebral quick-time. "Help, for heaven's sake, help!" she urged. ". . . We started out very well. The pieces I wrote . . . are the dough (half baked) . . . we need. If only I knew *what* to write, the form would take shape then and there. . . ." He helped her tackle theoretical problems in economics and politics, scrutinized her research, suggested topics. Sending him her articles, she would write, "I know you'll pick up the main thread immediately and add the finishing touches." Early on, her desire to reconcile love and work to fulfill his expectations heightened the intensity of their affair. "I feel the way you do," she wrote him on one of her frequent trips to Paris. "I dream about being near you, my only love. I struggle with myself, struggle hard, not to chuck the lectures and all the rest and come speeding to you. But I am ashamed. Besides, I feel, I know, that you will be more pleased with me after I've done all the things I should do."

Gradually their common work became fraught with conflict. Jogiches could never forgive or forget that it was through Luxemburg that he had become involved in the Polish movement. More important, his political existence was for years almost exclusively limited to supplying Luxemburg with ideas for her writing. "His brilliance and intelligence notwithstanding, Leo is simply unable to write," she later said. "The mere thought of putting his ideas on paper paralyzes him."[3] Actually it was the finality of being imprisoned in print that paralyzed him. Made public, his words could turn against him and prove his fallibility to the world. He operated from behind the scenes, avoiding daylight, avoiding people. He had no need for those he wanted to save. His one and only preoccupation was masterminding the party strategy that Luxemburg was expected to carry out. She resented it. "I'm just getting used to the idea," she wrote him, "that my only duty now is to think about the elections and later about what will happen after the elections. I feel like a forty-year-old woman going through the symptoms of menopause, although the two of us together are only about sixty years old." Or, resigned, she would say, ". . . I shifted to business—your style. It may be that you're right and that in another six months I'll turn at last into your ideal." It was the opposite of hers.

Writing for both of them, she soon found herself in an untenable position. "You think that for me it'll do to scribble articles . . . and follow your 'modest opinions,'" she wrote rebelliously. She agreed to his exercising his power through her but not to his arrogating power over her. She may have longed to be his little "Chuchya" in the privacy of their bedroom, but his attempts to control her mind as well as her every move vexed her. "If I'm independent enough to perform single-handed on the political scene, that independence must extend to buying a jacket." Her performance was rapidly becoming more single-handed than Jogiches could ever have wished.

Berlin was her stage. She descended upon the city like a colorful bird, elegant and brilliant. Although a woman—young, Jewish, and Polish—within three months, in 1898, she was offered the editorship of an important newspaper published by the powerful German Social Democratic Party.

Seasoned socialists August Bebel, Karl Kautsky, and Clara Zetkin befriended her. In her the opposition discovered a forceful adversary. Her courage and wit, her fiery oratory, and knife-edged pen captivated and shocked. Jogiches's share in her career was, as before, not negligible. His letters stimulated her thinking day by day: "In your last letter you gave me an entire piece for my article, which stands out like a jewel. . . ," she readily admitted, "I translated [it] from your letter word for word."

Once she had feared that her success might poison their relationship because of his pride and suspicions. Now, while lavishing assurances on him that the sole aim of her triumphs was to give him moral support, she basked happily in her new-found glory. "The divine," she was now called, and "the conqueror." But political success did not compensate for an unfulfilled personal life. The ecstasy she had shared with Jogiches tantalized her. His words, "There are no other hands like yours, delicate hands," kept coming back to her. Each day away from him was a new torment and a new reminder of past bliss. "I will never forget," she wrote to him in Zurich, how ". . . we held each other on the road in the darkness and looked at the crescent moon over the mountains . . . carried [groceries] upstairs together . . . the oranges, the cheeses . . . had such magnificent dinners . . . on the little table. . . . I still smell that night's air." The memory of happiness contrasting with her unwanted solitude filled her with real and imaginary fears. More than ever she longed for a home with him and a child by him.

But for two years Jogiches refused to join her. From Zurich he kept dispatching orders, advice, reprimands, through her "influencing history"—his ultimate dream. Resentful of the vicariousness of this experience, proud of her success, yet jealous of it, he feared her demands to "live openly as husband and wife." Only her ultimatum forced him to trudge to Berlin. A commander without troops, relegated to the role of prince consort, he now sat in their apartment reading her reports of her triumphant tours and unequaled popularity.

Nor was Luxemburg happy. "Real life" was still out of her reach. As a little girl she firmly believed that real life was hidden somewhere behind tall roofs. "Ever since, I've been trying to find it," she wrote after she had broken with Jo-giches, "but it always kept hiding behind one roof or other."[4] Her love was never wholly reciprocated. Jogiches continued to elude her. It was not, she realized, just geographic distance that divided them.

Jealous of his "inner life," she could not bear the thought that a part of him existed to which she had no access. "I feel an outsider," she protested and at the same time berated herself for the "torment" she inflicted on him by saying it. The realization that she herself, often unwittingly, injured his pride and made him suffer and withdraw, made her fight for Jogiches's soul more ferociously and more hopelessly, and it made him increasingly desperate to defend what was left of his being. He felt uneasy when she gave, unhappy when she did not, furious when she let him know that she was giving. He wanted her undivided attention, but he measured and directed it. Any intrusion upon territory he considered off limits he consistently and strictly forbade. He wanted her dependent, to keep her, and independent, to prove himself a genius-maker. Responsibility for her happiness or unhappiness he did not want, nor did he want to let go of it. When she was unhappy, he felt guilty; when she was happy, cheated.

The passage of time created a chasm between them. Her vision of herself and of Jogiches's place in her life differed when she was thirty and a celebrity from when she was twenty and unknown. Jogiches, in his mid-thirties, fully realized the gap between his youthful aspirations and the disappointments of reality. While her transition from youth to adulthood was marked by achievements and recognition, for him it was a farewell to dreams of power.

She wanted them to "live like other people," to have peaceful and orderly lives, although order and serenity were unattainable for either of them. Always, she wanted the impossible. In politics she fought for the revolution yet abhorred violence and bloodshed. It was typical of the contradictions in her nature to want thunder silent and a hurricane calm. She pushed and prodded him toward the unattainable "peaceful life," aware yet unmindful of his private hell. His constant agonizing, the malaise that was eating away at him, she saw as a "senseless, spiritual suicide." He was, she claimed, wasting himself for no reason but his "savage madness." In despair she turned to another man. And Jogiches, like the magician who lost control over the spirit he himself had created, felt he had lost his power and, therefore, lost her.

After their break became final, in 1907, they lived apart, separated but never strangers. All his attempts to win her back failed. There was suffering and rage, but the kinship survived. They continued to work together, their youthful dreams of social revolution untouched.

There were other affairs in her life, meaningless affairs. Perhaps she wanted to prove to Jogiches or to herself that, as she had once written him, "I don't need your love . . . I can live without it." But then, as later, she never really could. Years before, exasperated by his coldness, she had cried, "I could kill you!" She did not kill him. She went on, living an imitation of life until, in January 1919, she was assassinated. Two months later, hunting down her assassins, Jogiches too was murdered.

2

A woman and a Jew, Luxemburg personified two oppressed classes. She grew up at a time when both were beginning to stir restlessly.

The lot of women in Poland was similar to that in other European Roman Catholic countries. For centuries, reared in the virtues of submissiveness and humility, in dread of sin and punishment, their lives had been circumscribed by the feudal-patriarchal family. Depending upon her social status, a woman served either to combine adjoining estates by a suitable match or to produce offspring to till the soil. In folklore, and perhaps in reality, the first emancipated woman was a widow who, by poisoning her husband, had achieved financial and thereby personal independence.

In Poland, as in other European countries, industrialization undermined the established attitudes; power and money changed hands. The feudal elite—the Catholic Church and the hereditary nobility—saw the emergence of a new elite: the bourgeoisie. The impoverished aristocracy could no longer support chivalrous knights and romantic maidens. The man, hitherto privileged by birth and property, tried to compensate for his diminished influence by emphasizing his mental and physical superiority. His equally impecunious female counterpart was often reduced to the role of governess, or, to save the family from bankruptcy, was married off to a nouveau riche. The new leisure class, like the earlier one, used women as a means to amass ever bigger fortunes and to acquire a coveted coat of arms. Among the rising intelligentsia, slowly emerging competition for professional positions intensified the antagonism between the sexes. As members of the growing urban proletariat, women workers were the lowest of the low.

This regrouping of social classes included the Jews. Privileges and restrictions going back to the thirteenth century were modified in the mid-1800s. There was also an increase in migration from small towns and villages to urban centers. There, a few Jews achieved prominence in scholarship, professions, and wealth; many joined the ranks of the proletariat, and some the *lumpenproletariat*. The Luxemburg family, too, left a small town for Warsaw. Like many educated, assimilated Jews, they identified themselves with Poles and gave their children a modern education. Luxemburg's father was typical of those Jews who were sympathetic to the cause of Polish independence. Many of them supported the 1863 insurrection that brought further changes.

In that insurrection, sometimes called the "Women's War," women proved to be skilled conspirators and comrades-in-arms. Russian chroniclers who "attributed the frenzy of the resistance and the long, desperate fight to the dazzling eyes and high spirits of the Polish women," missed the vital point.[5] For two decades the vestals had been turning into warriors; they demanded recognition not only of their womanly virtues but also of their ability to think and to work. If their initial behavior—imitating men, condemning marriage, scorning public opinion—provoked disgust, they themselves were sufficiently disgusted with their position as "virgins," "dolls," or "angels," to challenge the Church, tradition, and society. Their tulle and velvet discarded, they revealed themselves as a power to be reckoned with.

Paradoxically, economic and political oppression accelerated the process of women's coming-of-age. For example, one of the first mass strikes in Warsaw erupted after women laborers and prostitutes had been ordered by the czarist police to undergo identical hygienic checkups. In spite of class differences, the similarities in their predicaments united women: Polish women, weary of the pressures of the Church, Jewish women, tired of being pariahs, came out of mansions and ghettoes to fight for personal independence. The battles were fought, too, on the pages of newspapers and novels. While Madame Bovary was victimized by her romantic notion of life, and Anna Karenina by her tragic passion, Marta (the protagonist of a famous novel by Eliza Orzeszkowa, published in 1873) paid with her life for being *useless in the labor market*. As racial prejudice in the case of

Jews, aggravated by the fear of economic competition, so sexual prejudice, in the case of women, less identifiable but equally insidious in the restrictions it imposed, dimmed hopes for progress. Education appeared—to women as to Jews—the way out of bondage. But education alone was not enough. Revolution—or socialism—seemed to Luxemburg's generation a panacea for all these ills.

The image of the woman-rebel was an integral part of Luxemburg's formative years. She was eight years old when Vera Zasulich walked into the office of General Trepov, governor of St. Petersburg, and fired at him at point-blank range. She was eleven when Sofia Perovskaia, the daughter of a Russian general, was executed for her part in the assassination of Czar Alexander II. At the time of Luxemburg's graduation from the gymnasium, the twenty-one-year-old Maria Bohusz, one of the leaders of the first Polish workers' party Proletariat, perished in Siberian exile. The same fate met the revolutionary Rosalia Felsenhardt, the daughter of a Jewish medic. Aleksandra Jentys, a woman of great intelligence and beauty and cofounder of Proletariat, was imprisoned with her lover, Ludwik Waryński, founder of the party. She was exiled; he died in a Russian dungeon.

In this rapidly changing society, however, the call to arms lost its appeal for many. Industrialization provided a chance for a different kind of action. The older generation saw that armed struggle bled the nation without weakening the Russian oppressor; cooperation with the Russians rather than rebellion, economic progress rather than hopeless bloodshed, seemed the realistic solution. But rebellion did not die. Long-haired young men and short-cropped young women, often sons and daughters of factory owners, appeared in the streets of Warsaw, shocking the burghers and infuriating the police. These young people were instrumental in showing the workers ways to assert their rights. The czarist authorities, joined by extreme Polish nationalists, tried to stop the Jews from

joining forces with revolutionary Poles but were only par-
tially successful. "Polish rebels" (*buntovshchiki*) were noto-
rious with the czarist police. Conspirators, recklessly coura-
geous, carrying daggers under their faddish cloaks, were
incorrigible and dangerous until hanging from the gallows.
They started their careers, boys and girls alike, at fourteen.
At seventeen they were full-fledged subversives; at nineteen
or twenty they cried from the gallows, "Long live Poland!"
"Long live socialism!" "Long live revolution!"

Czarist repression forced women, teachers and students,
into the underground. Schools turned into hotbeds of conspiracy where future revolutionaries received their basic
training. Whispered messages, secret glances, addresses exchanged in murky school corridors and on street corners,
arranged not only a romantic rendezvous but also illegal
classes. In the underground another "revolution" occurred—
in the attitudes of the sexes. Girls, though still chaperoned
to balls and teas, were now discovering comrades and friends
in their male fellow students. In the clandestine circles studying forbidden Polish literature and history and discussing
theories of social progress, young people learned the meaning of comradeship and free love. The emphasis Luxemburg
put on friendship in her relationship with Jogiches echoed
this spirit.

While in exile, Luxemburg first came to know the organized struggle for women's rights. In Germany socialists like
August Bebel and Clara Zetkin put that fight on an equal
footing with the fight for workers' rights. Luxemburg's ap-
proach was different. The belief that people should not be
divided by sex but united against the exploiters shaped her
views on women's emancipation. It was, from her point of
view, yet another harmful division, comparable to the divi-
sions by class, race, or nationality that split the international
proletariat. For the same reason, although other reasons also
played a role, she refused to support any separate Jewish

movement, even though her social consciousness and her uncompromising rejection of nationalism can be understood only in the light of Jewish emancipation. Once socialism had been won, she believed, women and Jews, like other oppressed people, would have all the rights which the capitalist system had denied them. This stand did not prevent her, however, from encouraging her women friends to assert their independence.

On the Jewish question, she remained intransigently consistent. Her own rise to power influenced her feelings: if she, a Jew, could achieve such prominence, anti-Semitism could not be a special social problem but merely one among the many manifestations of oppression inherent in capitalism. She disregarded the differences rooted in divergent cultural and social conditions. "To me," she wrote in 1917, "the poor victims of the rubber plantations in Putumayo, the Negroes in Africa . . . are equally close."[6] The Jewish peddler in a small Polish village is the same as a Colombian rubber plantation worker. For Luxemburg, he is no longer a specific, concrete human individual, a member of a historically shaped national and religious entity, but the pure essence of man. In brief, she did not feel that there were truly important distinctions in the situation of Jews, Africans, Latin Americans, or other Europeans. Whether and to what extent this attitude stemmed from her rejection of nationalism or from her own need to escape the confines of the "ghetto" into a nationless human community, it typified the illusion shared by some Jews before and after her.

The breach with Jogiches and the outbreak of World War I slightly modified Luxemburg's attitude toward women. Her unique success, and Jogiches's unwavering support, had spared her the common lot of her female contemporaries. When called the "Red Prima Donna" or the "Jewish Rose," she could afford nonchalantly to shrug off such slurs. The war, however, made her seek allies among women who were now fighting not their inferior status but its result—the lack of power. Isolated, with no political influence, women were unable to make decisions about themselves, their children, or their country. By this time Luxemburg knew this isolation. In 1915, she decided to participate in an International Women's Conference in Holland. Men, she realized, controlled the German Social Democratic Party. Under their leadership the party grew increasingly conservative, more interested in the worker's wages than in his political growth. Men held positions of power in the Socialist International and in their respective governments. Now, allying themselves with those who made wars and profited by them, they voted for war budgets. If in the past she had equated courage with manhood—"there are two men left in the party," she said back in 1907, "Clara Zetkin and I"—she now saw things differently. She would have smiled ironically at what her biographer intended as a compliment: "There was much that was *manly* about Rosa Luxemburg," he wrote, "in her keen intellect, in her boundless energy, in her dauntlessness, in her confidence and assertiveness."[7]

3

Since the 1920s the term "revolutionary" has undergone a change that Luxemburg and her peers might have seen as a monstrous caricature. Their concept of the aim of revolution was democracy and freedom, a social order that would liberate man from the arbitrary use of political and economic power. They differed as much from latter-day revolutionaries as their vision differed from its implementation. Dispersed throughout Europe, they worked toward the same goal—a more human and more humane society.

A unique group, they had no predecessors and hardly any successors. They were enlightened Europeans, many of them Jews, who appeared in the second half of the nineteenth century only to disappear with the advent of labor camps, concentration camps, purges, and gas ovens. In mind and spirit they were the obverse of those who today falsely claim their intellectual heritage. Selfless, incorruptible, civilized, they did not set out to "save" the world but to make it a better place to live in. They were not free of ambition, pettiness, intolerance; political intrigue was not beyond them, nor were personal squabbles. Personalities clashed, ideological battles were fought, but the foundations stood firm. Once, when the French socialist Jaurés delivered a fiery speech against Luxemburg's theories and there was no one to interpret for him, she stood up and translated his ardent oration into equally impassioned German. To paraphrase Leonard Woolf, they knew it was the disunity of the civilized, not the unity of the barbarians, that was dangerous to their cause. History has proved them right.

They neither desired nor sought power over the workers. An educated worker, they believed, would develop a sense of solidarity with workers the world over, would comprehend the pervasiveness and limitations of capitalism, and, once in power, would put an end to its rule. Like Marx before them, they failed to understand the worker's lack of pride in his status, his aspiration to achieve a higher social position, if not for himself at least for his children. "Citizens of the world," multilingual, equally at home in all the capitals of Europe, they projected their lofty ideals onto the mundane reality of the worker. They knew the art of living and dreamed of a social order of which the hitherto oppressed would partake. Not averse to the small luxuries of life, with a taste for music and literature and a deep attachment to Western civilization, they wanted to make that culture a need and a property of the "wretched of the earth."

Luxemburg's attitude toward personal happiness, which she saw as a natural human yearning, and that of Jogiches, who considered it antithetical to "the cause," reflect the difference between the group that lost and the one that won.

Bent on making people "happy" according to their recipe, the latter succeeded in having the world equate "revolution" with the denial of a life fulfilled and rich. "[I] hate 'asceticism' . . . more than ever," Luxemburg wrote from prison to Jogiches. "I keep grasping greedily at each spark of life, each glimmer of light . . . [and] promise myself *to live* life to its fullest as soon as I'm free."

Socialism was, for Luxemburg, a faith to which people should be educated, not forced. Marx considered socialism a historical necessity and asserted that the forces of history are moving toward social revolution, which he regarded as an end morally valid and therefore worth fighting for. After his death the so-called Marxists started to present Marx as a mere historical determinist, a simplistic believer in sociological laws. Luxemburg, in contradiction to this interpretation of Marx's writings, stressed an ethical dimension: the moral obligation to fight for a more humane social system. The progress of mankind is inevitably linked with moral virtue. *Realpolitik* is immoral and therefore worthless; it is also the parent of cowardice, which she regarded as the greatest of sins.

Marx's words, "moi, je ne suis pas Marxiste," fit well with her interpretation of Marxism. She conceived of it as a humanistic philosophy capable of restoring wholeness to man. The "Marxist jargon," which supplied fuel for demagogues and corrupted intellect, she found deceptive and dangerous. Marxism was not a dogma for her but a scientific tool to create new concepts and real changes. "Rosa Luxemburg" wrote Georg Lukács, "was the only disciple of Marx who effectively continued his life work in both economic theory and economic method."[8]

Answering Jogiches's misgivings about an article of hers, she said: "Your fear of my emphasizing our antagonism to Marx seems to me *unfounded*. Nobody will be appalled by it for the entire piece is nothing but a triumphant song of

Marxism." Equally opposed to Russian despotism and Prussian barrack drill, she brought to modern revolutionary
thought an almost mystical faith in the revolutionary poten-
tial of the workers, which no one was able to shake and few
were able to accept.

Luxemburg's assessment of Lenin and the Russian Revolution continues to provoke controversy. She is alternately
presented and interpreted as a Marxist heretic and a Marxist
orthodox. Best known in the West as a critic of the revolution,
she is extolled in the East as its forerunner and supporter.
Her analysis of the October Revolution (written in 1918),
dismissed as a momentary delusion by some and hailed as
prophetic by others, is neither. It is a logical continuation of
her philosophy, based on the concept of dynamic rather than
static history and on the inevitability of moving toward a
more advanced, that is, a more democratic, society. She welcomed the revolution, stating that Lenin's was "the sole party
in Russia that grasped the true interest of the revolution in
that first period [. . .]" However, she felt Lenin's and Trotsky's remedy, the complete elimination of democracy, was
"worse than the disease it was supposed to cure. . . ." She
wrote, "Socialism, by its very nature, cannot be dictated,
introduced by command. . . . [Lenin] is completely mistaken
in the means he employs: decree, the dictatorial power of a
factory overseer, draconic penalties, rule by terror—all these
are means preventing rebirth. . . . Without general elections,
without unrestricted freedom of press and assembly, without
a free exchange of opinions, life dies out in every public
institution and only bureaucracy remains active. . . . Slowly,
public life falls into sleep, and a few dozen party leaders . . .
command and rule. . . . In reality the power is executed by
a dozen outstanding minds while the elite of the working
class are now and then invited to meetings in order to ap-
plaud the speeches of the leaders and to approve unanimously proposed resolutions. In fact, then, it is a clique—

certainly a dictatorship, not, however, the dictatorship of the proletariat but that of a handful of politicians. . . ." She emphasized that Lenin and his comrades "have contributed to the cause of international socialism whatever could possibly have been contributed under such fiendishly difficult conditions. However, the danger begins," she pointed out, "with their making a virtue of necessity. . . ." She stated, "Freedom only for the supporters of the government, only for the members of one party, no matter how numerous, is no freedom. Freedom is always freedom for the one who thinks differently."[9]

She did not believe that one party could have the monopoly on wisdom. And she rejected the principle of centralization, which she saw as "simply taking the conductor's baton out of the hands of the bourgeoisie and putting it into the hands of a socialist Central Committee."[10]

Luxemburg's insistence on linking politics with morality never ceased to embarrass socialists on the right and on the left; it spelled her political downfall. On both sides of the barricade, revolutionaries and conservatives, her political friends and enemies, breathed a sigh of relief at her assassination. But she would not die—*non omnis moriar*. She alone among her contemporaries made a comeback in the 1960s as tanks rolled and shots were fired and people were fighting again for government "with a human face." For whenever it is time, to use Thoreau's words, "for honest men to rebel and revolutionize," Rosa Luxemburg's ideas return.

1. Quoted by Franco Venturi in *Roots of Revolution* (New York: Grosset & Dunlap, 1966), p. 366.
2. Quoted in Róża Luksemburg, *Listy do Leona Jogichesa-Tyszki*, F. Tych, ed. (Warsaw: Książka i Wiedza, 1968), vol. I., p. XXVII.
3. Ibid., p. XXXVIII.
4. Rosa Luxemburg, *Briefe an Karl und Luise Kautsky*, Luise Kautsky, ed. (Berlin: E. Laub'sche Verlagsbuchhandlung GmbH., 1923), p. 71.

5. Maria Zmigrodzka, *Orzeszkowa* (Warsaw: Państwowy Instytut Wydawniczy, 1965), p. 54.

6. Rosa Luxemburg, *Briefe an Freunde*, B. Kautsky, ed. (Hamburg: Europäische Verlaganstalt, GmbH, 1950), pp. 48-49.

7. Paul Frölich, *Rosa Luxemburg: Her Life and Work* (first edition, 1939; New York: Monthly Review Press, 1972), p. 187 (my italics).

8. Georg Lukács, *Geschichte und Klassenbewusstsein* (Berlin: Der Malik-Verlag, 1923), pp. 5-6.

9. Rosa Luxemburg, *Die Russische Revolution*, P. Levi, ed. (Berlin: Verlag Gesellschaft und Erziehung, GmbH, 1922), pp. 77-118.

10. Róża Luksemburg, *Wybór Pism* (Warsaw: Książka i Wiedza, 1959), vol. I, p. 341.

The Letters

The First Years
1893–1897

Rosa Luxemburg was born on March 5, 1870, in Zamość, a small town in Poland under Russian rule. The youngest child of Elias Luxemburg and Lina Löwenstein, she had a sister, Anna, and three brothers, Mikolaj, Maksymilian, and Józef. Polish and German culture permeated the family's life. The Luxemburgs had no connections with the Jewish community of Zamość, which was one of the most cultured in Poland. When they moved to Warsaw in 1873, they left nothing behind—no ties, no regrets. Elias Luxemburg, a well-educated merchant, identified himself with the Polish patriots who, in two unsuccessful insurrections (1830 and 1863), sought to overthrow the hated czarist regime. Lina Luxemburg, a cultivated descendant of a long line of rabbis, was enamored of German poetry and music. Each parent leaned toward a different way of shedding Jewishness, although neither way was mutually exclusive.

As a small child, Rosa suffered from a hip disease that, wrongly diagnosed, left her with a permanent limp. Her older sister also limped; the three brothers were unusually handsome and attractive.[1] Injustice, perhaps first symbolized by the injustice of nature, concerned her from an early age. "My ideal is a social system that allows one to love everybody with a clear conscience. Striving after it, defending it, I may perhaps even learn to hate," wrote the teenage schoolgirl. When Rosa graduated from the Second Girls Gymnasium in Warsaw at the age of seventeen, she was not a stranger to the socialist movement. It electrified girls and boys who had their eyes open to the humiliation and injustice rampant in a Warsaw starting on the road to industrialization: the squalor of the first generation of factory workers, the brutality of the czarist police putting down strikes, the emergence of the new leisure class.

Two years later, in 1889, to escape the czarist police, Luxemburg fled to Switzerland, never to return to Warsaw, except for a few months sixteen years later. In Geneva she met the legendary Vera Zasulich, who as a young girl shot at General Trepov and G. V. Plekhanov, the famous Russian Marxist theorist. And she met Leo Jogiches.

"Light of my life, my sun," she writes in one of her early letters to him, ". . . the night is so dark, the mountains close in on me, huge, massive, the stars shine, unfriendly, and a cold wind blows. All around there is dead silence. And I am again alone, all alone." They met in 1890 when Luxemburg was twenty and Jogiches was twenty-three. In 1893 they founded the first influential Polish Marxist workers' party, the Social Democracy of the Kingdom of Poland (SDKP).[2]

Leo Jogiches came to Switzerland from Lithuania. Wilno, its capital, was a unique conglomeration of Lithuanians, Poles, and Jews, each a rich cultural force strenuously fighting Russification—a struggle in which socialism and revolution had a particular appeal. Jogiches was born in 1867 into a wealthy and prominent family. The house of his grandfather, Jakub, was the meeting place of the Wilno intelligentsia. His father, Samuel, died when the boy was young. Leo worshipped his mother, Zofia, and she was to remain the only sustaining force in his life. After her death in 1898, he wrote to Luxemburg, ". . . now there is no one left at home," a telling confession considering that his sister, Emilia, and his two brothers, Józef and Paweł, were still living in Wilno. Jogiches left the gymnasium to become a worker and to devote himself to revolution. Imprisoned for several months in 1888 for his revolutionary activities, he escaped abroad in 1890. His independent income put him in a privileged position. He could afford to buy a printing press, to finance party publications, to support Luxemburg. Money was always to be a problem in their relationship and is a recurrent theme in the letters. It took on both a symbolic and a psychological significance of domination and submission.

In Switzerland, cut off from day-to-day conspiratorial work, unable to reach an agreement with Russian political exiles, Jogiches got involved in the Polish movement through Luxemburg. He was a member of the Central Committee of the SDKPiL which, until 1914, was his only practical sphere of activity. The modest scope of the party (200 members in 1893) could hardly satisfy his political ambitions. Between 1890 and 1897, both were students at the University of Zurich, living apart but within walking distance of each other. In 1893, the twenty-three-year-old woman created a sensation at the Third Congress of the Socialist International with her first public speech. A year later she became editor in chief of the SDKP organ *The Workers' Cause* [*Sprawa Robotnicza*]. The paper was printed in Paris where Luxemburg was also doing research on her doctoral dissertation. Here she established long-lasting relationships with luminaries of French socialism, Jean Jaurès, Jules Guesde, and Edouard Vaillant. Her home was still in Zurich with Jogiches, with whom she occasionally spent working vacations in some small Swiss village.

1. A few months before she died in 1977, Luxemburg's niece, Halina Luxemburg-Więckowska, the daughter of Maksymilian, generously shared her family memories with me.
2. In 1900 SDKP was reorganized as the Social Democracy of the Kingdom of Poland and Lithuania (SDKPiL). (See appendix.)

Two young exiles—Rosa Luxemburg from Poland

Leo Jogiches from Lithuania

High school student in Warsaw: "My ideal is a social system that allows one to love everybody with a clear conscience. Striving after it, defending it, I may perhaps even learn to hate."

Letter 1

[Clarens, Switzerland]
[March 21, 1893]

A voice in the night woke me. Startled, I listened. It was my own words I heard, "Dyodyo! Hey, Dyodyo!"[1] I was pulling the bedclothes toward me, irritably, thinking my Dyodyo was there beside me (what an indecent dream!). When I couldn't move the bedclothes I murmured angrily, "silly Dyodyo, just you wait till morning!" After my voice brought me to my senses, I knew it was a dream, and I knew the sad truth—my Dyodyo was far, far away, and I was all, all alone. Just then I heard footsteps on the stairs. Half asleep I figured out it was *you*; you managed to catch the last train (in my dream I slightly changed the timetable). You didn't want to wake me up, went to sleep upstairs, and were going to surprise me in the morning. I smiled happily and fell asleep. In the morning I rushed upstairs only to see that my night's vision was merely a dream. If you don't come by Wednesday, I'll catch the first train to Geneva. Beware!

1. Dyodyo or Dyodya, a caressing, intimate diminutive, coined either by his family when Leo Jogiches was a child or by L. Angry with him, she wrote, "My dear, 'Dyodya' you beg me for, you no longer deserve, and I don't know how soon you will. . . ." January 7, 1902.

Letter 2

[Paris]
Sunday 3:30 P.M.
[March 25, 1894]

My Dear! I've been very angry with you. I must bring up some ugly things you did. I was so hurt that I had decided not to write at all for the rest of my stay here. But my feelings won out. This is what I hold against you:

1. Your letters contain *nothing, but nothing* except for *The Workers' Cause,* criticism of what I have done, and instructions about what I should do.[1] If you answer indignantly that you never fail to say tender things in your letters to me, let me tell you that *sweet talk* is not what I want. You can have it. I want you to write me about your personal life. But not a single word! Our only ties are the Cause and the memory of old feelings. This is very painful. I realized it here with particular clarity. When, totally exhausted by the never-ending Cause, I sat down to catch my breath, I looked back and realized I don't have a home anywhere. I neither exist nor live as *myself.* In Zurich it is the same, or rather still more annoying, editorial work. I don't want to stay here or go back to Zurich. Don't tell me I can't stand the never-ending work, that all I want is some rest. No, no, I can stand twice as much but what I can't stand is that wherever I turn, there's only one thing—"The Cause." It's boring, draining. Why should everybody pester me when I give it all I can? It's a burden—every letter, from you or anyone else, always the same—this issue, that pamphlet, this article or that. Even that I wouldn't mind if *besides, despite* it, there was a *human being* behind it, a soul, an individual. But for you there's nothing, nothing but "The Cause." Have you had no experiences all this time? No ideas? No books? No impressions? Nothing to share with me?! Possibly you'd like to ask me the same questions? Unlike you, I have impressions and ideas all the time, the *"Cause"* notwithstanding. But with whom am I supposed to share them? With you? Oh, no, I've too much pride. I'd share them with Heinrich, with Mitek [Hartman][2] with Warski,[3] but alas, I don't love them and don't feel like doing it. I do love you but—I suppose I'm repeating myself.

It's not true that right now you're pressed for time. There's always something to talk about and time to write. It all depends on one's attitude. Here's a typical example for you—and my second objection. Let's say that you indeed live only

by our and your cause. Just take the Russian cause. Did you
write me a single word about it? What's going on, what's
being published, how are those people in Zurich? No, it didn't
occur to you to write me anything about it. I know nothing
special has happened; still, one writes about small unimportant things to someone close. But you think that for me it will
do to scribble articles for [*The Workers'*] *Cause* and to follow
your "modest opinions" to the dot.

Very Characteristic.

3. Another example. Hein[rich] went to Zurich. As I learned
from his letter, he told you about the whole affair, and he discussed it with you, and you *insisted* on changes in the organizational relations between [*The Workers'*] *Cause* and the
party. Without telling me a word? Without my opinion? Without telling me anything, you make and *push* your decisions?
At least H[einrich] was honest enough to write and ask for my
opinion. You never did.

4. I found out from Brzez[ina's] letter that he instructed
Heinrich to tell me about the situation on the frontier.[4] Of
course Heinrich informed you at once, but you didn't tell me
a word. I'm sitting here, rushing the work, shipping the paper,
with no idea whether there is any frontier, whether and how
much will reach its destination, how soon, who's doing
what—Brz[ezina] or Hein[rich]. All this is regarded as informa-
tion I can live without.

Your magnanimous advice not to *bother* about practical
matters, they'll be taken care of without me, could only be
given by somebody who *doesn't know me at all*. Such advice,
"Don't bother, your nerves are too weak," would just do for
Marchlewski.[5] For me such an attitude (even with the "sweet-
heart" thrown in) is insulting, to say the least. On top of it,
your directions are as frequent as they are crude: do this or
that with Warski, at Lavrov's behave this or that way, stick to
this or to that.[6] In the end I get an intense sense of distaste,
weariness, fatigue, and impatience which overcomes me when

I have time to think. I'm not telling you this because I bear a grudge. I can't *demand* that you be what you are not. I'm writing partly because I still have the stupid habit of telling you what I feel and partly because I want you to be aware of what's going on between us.

Attached are the proofs of all articles, except for Marchlewski's and the feuilleton. I didn't get the proofs of Marchlewski's article, but I rewrote it, so don't worry. The feuilleton, you know. Krichevsky's isn't set yet.[7] I'll go over it today.

I'm sending you the proofs because I'm slightly tired and don't have a clear grasp and I fear your reproaches. Look it over and jot down your notes. There's enough space. I didn't look at the proofs or correct the spelling, but don't bother, just look at the content. Krichevsky's article took up three columns, so one sheet just wouldn't do. The issue would have been flat because the article about the fight for shorter working hours, although superficial, took up a lot of space. See if you can cut it. I'll add some facts to the article about *our own* struggle and its effects, and I'll change the ending to make a transition to the struggle for an eight-hour day. What do you think about introducing it with a small piece signed "Ch"? (It is Defnet's article,[8] translated by Jadzia [Chrzanowska-Warska],[9] and corrected by me.) Warski says it won't do—he thinks a proclamation signed by the editors is a proper introduction. What do you think? I like this piece well enough to use it as an introduction.

We'll be left with seven empty columns in the double sheet. We can put in an article about women—one column—another about wages—one or one and a half—and I'll have to write an article on politics. That worries me most because I can't think of anything. Of course I'll write it, no matter what. I'll keep it short, two or two and a half columns. In the remaining space I'll put a short piece about preparations abroad for May 1st, emphasizing three points: (1) the English shifted the ceremony from Sunday to the exact day May 1st falls on; (2) the Germans agreed to *celebrate* it; (3) all French socialists joined to celebrate May 1st *together* for the first time. It will make the issue attractive and complete. You probably won't be delighted with Warski's article about May 1, but I cannot make it perfect. The poor man wrote it, I turned it down and outlined it for him, he rewrote it as I suggested. Then I revised and corrected it twice and I can't ask more of him. It's not bad now.

Tell me frankly what you think about the articles. No need to sweeten your comments on my articles with compliments that are distasteful. To make the article about working hours more readable, I'll break it into separate parts according to countries. I'll have the whole cut and fastened, and it will be easier to turn the pages. I didn't like Krichevsky's article—I'd rather write one myself, but I'll try to rewrite it. Your comments agree with mine more or less.

Now I'd like to ask you the following questions:

1. Is it all right to say that in 1848 the French people fought mainly for general elections?
2. Did the Chicago demonstration take place in 1886 or 1887?
3. How many rubles to a dollar? [. . .]
4. Did the strikes of the gas workers and longshoremen in England break out in 1889 and was it for an eight-hour day?

You'll certainly spot other questionable points.—Today's Sunday. You should get this letter with the proofs tomorrow, on Monday. Check promptly and get them back to me on Tuesday, at the latest on Wednesday, because on Tuesday I'll be finished with the articles (Warski is writing about the wages).—I was on Reiff's back till he hired one more typesetter, a Pole, and now he screams for the material.[10]

Enclosed is Reiff's receipt and the bills. Together with the 100 [francs] I got today, I have 118 for the cause. The brochure costs 90 or 100. (Paper is expensive; I think 7 Fr for one thousand small sheets and stitching.) What's left I'll keep for

myself. Unfortunately I'm spending a lot of money, don't know
how. The rent is 28 Fr, service at least 5—payable two weeks
in advance, so I paid 16. I pay Jadzia 1.50 a day (she feeds
me lunch and supper) so it makes altogether 23 Fr. It comes to
40 and I brought 60 and some change. It slipped through my
fingers, don't know how: a lamp—1.50; cocoa—1.20; milk—
1.65; Jadzia made me a hat for 2.25; gloves—2; sugar and
bread for breakfast about 2 Fr. What happened to the rest? No
idea. I spent 1 franc or 1½ for flowers and pastry for Jadzia
because she loves it (I don't eat any) and after all she spends a
lot of time cooking for me. Perhaps Warski took a few francs,
and something went wrong with the bills. Anyway, I'm penniless and must take about 18 from the money for the cause. I'll
be more careful from now on. The money you sent got here so
late that you must soon send about 125 for the February issue.
Remember, it will be ready on Wednesday. To save on postal
fees can you add some money for my expenses and my fare
back home?

As for sightseeing in Paris, I doubt that I should go anywhere. The dreadful noise and the crowds make me faint and
give me headaches. After half an hour in Bon Marché, I hardly
made it to the street.

The celebration of the [Paris] Commune was poor. Lafargue,
Paula Mink, Zévaès, Chauvin, and some others made
speeches. Very shallow, in particular Lafargue's. Guesde promised to come but didn't.[11] There were perhaps 200 people.
(Apparently there were more at the celebration jointly organized by all parties, but because of my nerves I was afraid to
go.)

I must stop—it's getting late for the mail. You don't consider
it necessary to send me newspapers, do you? You know very
well that the French newspapers print nothing but Parisian trivia. I've no idea what's going on in Germany and in Austria.
It's strange that you didn't think of it. Is Anna still in bed—isn't
she any better?[12] I'd certainly have written to her but *have no*

time. Did you get the (400) issues? Did you get the pamphlet, and what's wrong with it?

How large should the edition of the February issue be [of *The Workers' Cause*]? Where and how many copies should be sent?

What's the matter with the German proclamation, it is *urgent*! And what about the Polish—there's no way I can do it.

I mailed the brochure to Krichevsky. Did he like it? Did Anna?

Shipped off 2000 brochures to Munich. What do you want me to do with the remainder?

Had a letter from Mozhdzh[ensky]; it probably won't work.[13]

"Read my letter carefully" and answer *all* questions.[14]

1. *The Workers' Cause* [*Sprawa Robotnicza*], party organ of the Social Democracy of the Kingdom of Poland from 1894 to 1896 (see appendix), printed in Paris and smuggled into Russian-annexed Poland. L. was editor in chief after 1894.
2. Władysław Heinrich and Mieczysław Hartman, Poles studying in Zurich, closely connected with the SDKP.
[*In her letters L. refers to one and the same person by the first or the last name, initials, diminutives, etc. For the sake of clarity, the last name only is used in the translation.*]
3. Adolf Warszawski-Warski (1868-1937), a leading organizer of the Polish workers movement, cofounder of the SDKP and the SDKPiL, and in 1918 of the Polish Communist Party. He perished in Stalin's purges and was rehabilitated in 1956.
[*Some of the victims of Stalin's terror, falsely accused of counter-revolutionary activities, were posthumously rehabilitated after Stalin's crimes were publicly revealed.*]
4. Karol Brzezina, a go-between, smuggling *The Workers' Cause* to Poland.
5. Julian Marchlewski (1866-1925), economist, journalist, active in the Polish and international workers movements, cofounder of SDKPiL, and in 1919 co-organizer of the Communist International.
6. Piotr Lavrov (1823-1900), Russian emigrant, leading theorist of the Russian Populists (*Narodniki*).
7. Boris N. Krichevsky, Russian emigrant, a social democrat, journalist associated with *The Workers' Cause*.

8. Alfred Defnet, a Belgian socialist.
9. Jadwiga Chrzanowska-Warska, wife of Adolf Warski.
10. Adolf Reiff, a Polish printer, owner of a printing house in Paris.
11. Paul Lafargue, cofounder of Parti Ouvrier Français, married to Marx's daughter, Laura. Paula Mink, a Polish woman active in the Paris Commune. Alexandre Zévaès and René Chauvin, members of Parti Ouvrier Français. Jules Guesde, with Lafargue, cofounder of Parti Ouvrier Français.
12. Anna Gordon, Russian emigrant from Wilno and a close friend of Jogiches.
13. Gabriel Mozhdzhensky, Russian emigrant, socialist.
14. L. sometimes quotes J. back to tease him. Her quotation marks have been retained.

Letter 3

[Paris]
Thursday night
[April 5, 1894]

Beloved, my one and only treasure!

Here I am in my hotel, sitting in front of the table, trying to work on the proclamation. Dyodyu, my own! I don't feel like working!! My head's splitting, the street is rattling with dreadful noise, the room is horrid. . . . I can't stand it! I want to be back with you! Just think—I have to stay here for at least two more weeks. Because of the proclamation, I can't prepare my lecture this Sunday so it has to wait till the next—then the Russian lecture, and afterward I have to go and see Lavrov.

Dyodyu! Will there ever be an end to it? I'm beginning to lose my patience, and it isn't about the work but about you! Why haven't you come here! If I could kiss your sweet mouth now, I wouldn't be scared of any work. Baby, today at the Warskis, in the midst of discussing the proclamation, I felt such weariness in my soul and such longing for you that I almost started to scream. I fear that the old demon—the one from Geneva and Bern—will pounce on me one of these nights and lead me straight to the Gare de l'Est to Dyodyo, to my Dyodyo, to my Chuchya, to my whole world, to my whole life!!

To cheer myself up, I imagine myself going to you; I'm saying goodbye to the Warskis, the engine whistles, the train pulls out, and I'm off. Dear God, I feel as though the whole Alpine mountain range separated me from you. Dyodyu, when the train pulls into Zurich, you'll be waiting for me, and I'll scramble out of the train and rush to the entrance where you'll be standing in the crowd. But you mustn't run to me, I'll run to you!

We won't kiss at once or anything else, this would spoil everything, and say nothing. We'll walk quickly home, looking at each other, you know how, and smiling at each other. At home we'll sit down on the sofa and embrace, and I'll burst into tears just as I am doing now.

Dyodyo, I can't wait! I want it now! My golden one, I can't stand it any longer. To make things worse, afraid of a search, I destroyed your letters and am left with nothing to comfort me. Dyodyushky, let me kiss your sweet mouth and the tip of your nose! May I touch it with my little finger? You won't chase the cat out of the room again? Promise?

Your Polish is awful, do you know that?[1] Your wife will teach you a lesson, just wait! You'll probably be angry—not a word about business in the whole letter.

Well then, to make you feel better here's something: I like your proclamation very much except for a few short phrases. If this undercover agent is really in Zurich, try to get hold of him and worm that ill-fated issue of [*The Workers'*] *Cause* out of him. Should be easy.

Won't Wład[ysław Heinrich] wire the results?

Friday. I received money, books, and letters. Am working on the proclamation. Keep well and write.

Send me the issue of *Atheneum*[2] with the tariffs and the clippings Janek [Bielecki][3] had.

1. J's mother tongue was Russian. L. insisted that he learn Polish, which he came to know very well. He wrote to her in Russian, she to him in Polish. Making plans for their life together, she wrote, "Your Russian scares me out of my wits. . . . My Leon should speak Polish with me, but then you 'won't feel at home.' What shall we do? Your suggestion to speak both Polish and Russian at home is horrifying." June 1900.
2. A literary magazine published in Warsaw.
3. Jan Bielecki, Polish social democrat, chemistry student in Zurich.

Letter 4

[Paris]
Thursday night
[March 21, 1895]

My beloved, my own, dearest Dyodyo!

At last I can get some rest. I'm exhausted physically and spiritually. Finally, for the first time since I arrived, I'm alone, and I just moved into my new place. I have a lovely room, almost a little salon, and I dream of your coming here and of our being together (you could have a room in the same building). It's close to the Warskis but very far from the library, still a better location was out of the question for less than 50 to 75 francs.[1] It's cheaper to go to the library once a day by streetcar. I'll go in the morning and later have a homemade lunch nearby with a family of Polish social democrats where only Warski eats. Then I'll return to the library and at night go back home. The library is open from 9 A.M. to 5 P.M. But never mind these details.

My one and only, in my imagination I'm holding you close, my head on your shoulder, my eyes closed, resting. I'm worn out! And you, poor dear, now that you've more time, you've probably started working on your pamphlet. You've so little time! How is your work going?

How well I know you. Because of this letter you'll write me a tender one, and when I send you a cold letter, I'll get a cold one in return. You imitate everything I do, you never have a mood of your own unless you're furious and nasty. Why? Are we in the same situation? Must my impressions be yours? Why do you keep imitating me? Sometimes it really seems to me you're made of stone. Once it was done—proved in word and deed—that you love me, you *acted* like you loved me. But inside you, you feel nothing, no natural impulse to love. Oh, you horrid creature, I don't want you. [. . .]

Such enormously big parcels will immediately make the Warskis' concierge suspicious.[2] To have them sent to me is out of the question. An undercover agent visits my concierge regularly (write to me cautiously, coded when necessary, as you write to Brzezina, and spell my name with an *x* and an *m*)[3] and besides, that bitch of a concierge may herself denounce me. Thinking it over, I see that the paper *must* be shipped to you in Zurich. I can't ask Reiff to pack it the way you do because they never do it *that* way, they don't know how, and, as usual, they'll do a sloppy job. You must do it yourself with Marchlewski. Write back *at once* if you agree to having it sent to Zurich.

Now see how mean you are. I sense that every word concerning the most stupid business is twice, no ten, a hundred times more interesting to you than my pouring out my whole heart to you. Mention the PPS [Polish Socialist Party], and your eyes light up. Write about myself, that I'm tired, that I miss you, and it's quite different.

Well, I'm going to be strict! I mean it. I've been thinking about our relationship, and once I'm back I'll take you so firmly in hand that you'll squeal. Just wait and see! I'm going to terrorize you mercilessly. You must humble yourself, give in, bend, if our relationship is to continue. I must break you, tame you, or I won't put up with you any longer. You're an angry man, and, having finally figured you out, I'm as sure of it as that night follows day. I'll wipe that anger out of you, so help me God. I've the right to do it because I'm ten times better than you and, because I'm aware of it, I've all the more right to condemn this trait in you. I'll terrorize you without pity till you soften and have feelings and treat other people as any simple, decent man would. I love you above anything else in the world and at the same time have no mercy for your faults. So remember and watch out! I've gotten myself a rug beater and will start to beat you the minute I get home.

I know all this doesn't make much sense to you, but I'll explain when I see you. To start my reign of terror—remember, *be good*! Write tender, good letters, have a little humility, deign to tell me that you love me. Don't be afraid of humiliating yourself. You gave me three cents' worth more love today than I gave you yesterday. So what? Don't be afraid and ashamed to show your feelings out of fear that I won't be responsive enough. That is, if you *have* feelings. If you *don't*, I can't force anything. Learn to kneel spiritually, not only when I call you with open arms but also when I turn my back on you. In brief, be generous, lavish, squander your love on me. I demand it! Unfortunately your constant company is ruining my character, but this makes me even more eager to fight you. Remember, you *must* surrender because the might of my love will conquer you anyhow. My own, keep well, I hold you in my arms and cover you with kisses.

Darlingest, *please send me some money for my expenses!* At once.[4]

You'll get caviar for me from Rostov (my brother's gift). Crazy, aren't they? Don't you dare to touch it, save it for Weggis!!

You rascal, send me your picture *at once*!

Send my mail *promptly*.

My address: Avenue Reille 7, au 3-ème.

1. L. was doing research in Paris for her doctoral dissertation "The Industrial Development of Poland." She obtained her *Doctor Juris Publici et Rerum Cameralium* at the University of Zurich in 1897. A rare distinction, the dissertation was published in book form (see letters 9 and 12).
2. The parcels contained copies of *The Workers' Cause.*
3. In Polish, L.'s name was spelled Luksemburg or Luksenburg.
4. On September 14, 1899, L. wrote to J., "My dear, do me a favor and stop underlining words in your letters; it sets my teeth on edge. The whole world is not full of idiots who, as you think, understand only when bashed over the head with a club."

Letter 5

[Paris]
Thursday morning
March 28 [1895]

My dearest dear, my only one! I'm rushing, hurrying to you, I need rest, I need to talk to you. I am so tired! Why? It's Paris and being separated from you. I'm so weak—after only four hours in town, getting on and off the streetcars—I'm dizzy with fatigue. Back home I lie down for two hours, completely empty, like a corpse—pale, like ice—cold. Consequently, there's little time left to do anything, or to write. This is my day: I get up at 8:30 (Wojnarowska wakes me up at 8),[1] I wash, brush my teeth, shine my shoes (a shoeshine isn't included in the service, and if I hinted that it should be, the concierge would be insulted), brush my dress and hat, get dressed, have tea, do my accounts for the previous day, put papers in order for Reiff and Goupy, etc. Unfortunately all this takes till noon. Then I usually pick up Jadzia and have lunch with her. The round trip takes more than an hour, lunch another hour. If I have to discuss business with Reiff and Goupy, it gets to be 5 or 6 P.M. because they live miles away; even the streetcar takes half an hour to get there. Reiff, that idiot, needs at least two hours to get anything done. Then I go back home and for an hour lie there completely empty. After that Wojnarowska

feeds me a hot dinner, which means at least an hour because
she loves to talk. Since she's doing me a favor, I can't treat her
like a restaurant, just eat and run.

By then it's 8 P.M., and I've only three hours left because by
11 my eyes just won't stay open and I must go to bed. [. . .]
I'm somehow dulled and sleepy all the time and couldn't write
anything new even if I had the time. That's why I've been
doing the mechanical work and putting off writing until
"later," like that article about *The Worker*. I suppose I'm hoping for the holy ghost to descend and grant me inspiration.
[. . .]

I still haven't settled the overdue accounts with Warski because I see very little of him. Enclosed is my account for the
450 Fr you gave me. I spent 371.50 on printing—you have the
bills; I'm left with 58.50, and 20, I'm ashamed to confess, I
borrowed. My golden one, my own, don't be angry at the de-
tailed account of my personal expenses. Our relationship is so
wonderful now that it isn't a matter of feeling dependent or
anything like that, I just wanted to tell you about the expenses
because they shocked me too. Only after adding them up did I
realize what happened. See, on my regular expenses I spent
little or at least not *that* much. The only extra expense was for
the [Paris] Commune celebration. The deficit was caused by
two extra big expenses: I lent Jadzia 30 Fr and spent 24 at Bon
Marché. Jadzia will *definitely* return the 30 (remember, last
time the Warskis returned 20 Fr). The 24 I spent is your own
fault. To please you I bought some reasonably decent things:
clothes brush 2.50, a mirror 3 Fr, etc. Only because of you, I
swear, I bought things that are pleasant to touch and pleasant
to look at. Whenever I can, I get something nice to decorate
our room or to keep myself clean and pretty. All this costs
money, my dearest, at least in the beginning. For instance, I
bought a mirror the size of this letter paper, a nice wooden
frame, good quality glass. I did it *only* because you're always
busy primping in front of the mirror, so now you'll have a

pretty one on your dressing table. We'll also have a lovely tray
under the coffee pot and glasses, and another one for bread.

You may be amazed I spent all that money, but I want to
collect as many things as I can now so that our place won't
look the way it did before. And our entire regime is going to
change. We'll go to bed and get up *regularly* and *early,* we'll
dress nicely, the room will be elegant, and we'll have plenty
of our own things, and *there'll be no fights* (watch out!) because I want to be healthy and pretty and so do you. These
fights turn our whole life upside down. We'll work regularly
and peacefully. I'll agree to all your demands concerning my
looks and our home (*not* my relations with *people,* however!),
but, remember, two things have to go: fights and irregular
sleeping hours. You'd better prepare yourself because this time
I have made up my mind to start living like a human being,
and should you frustrate my plans, I'll hang myself. Our relationship, too, is bound to change if our daily life is peaceful
and regular. Remember! The *first* time you make a scene, on
my honor, I'll *run away* from you. Not with an officer—alone!
Honestly, I don't see another way.

My precious, listen, what do you think about buying three
decent silverplated spoons, knives, and forks? I get sick at the
thought of our black greasy forks and the rusty tin knives.
Since we spend so much money anyhow, we might as well
live half decently.

My golden one, I do understand and feel what you need
and what, apart from all else, gets on your nerves, and I'll try
to fix up the place nicely, to make it our *own,* to end this
mess. Still, the mess is no excuse for your scenes; on the contrary, it's all *your* fault—when I'm alone, I live an orderly life,
I keep the place neat and think about how to make it pretty.
And why? Because I'm not constantly frantic, disheartened,
driven crazy by you. Be good, and I'll do my best to make us
a nice home. Only be good and love me, and then

everything'll be fine. My own, write often! My golden dearest dear, I have much more to tell you. Till I see you!

Your own R.

1. Cezaryna Wanda Wojnarowska, a prominent Polish woman and socialist living in Paris and, until 1904, representative of the SDKPiL in the International Socialist Bureau.

Letter 6

[Switzerland]
[July 16, 1897]

No, I can't work anymore. I can't stop thinking of you. I must write to you. Beloved, dearest, you're not with me, yet my whole being is filled with you. It might seem irrational to you, even absurd, that I'm writing this letter—we live only ten steps apart and meet three times a day—and anyway, I'm only your wife—why then the romanticism, writing in the middle of the night to my own husband?[1] Oh, my golden heart, let the whole world think me ridiculous, but not you. Read this letter seriously, with feeling, the same way you used to read my letters back in Geneva when I wasn't your wife yet. I'm writing with the same love as then; my whole soul goes out to you as it did then, and now, as then, my eyes fill with tears (here probably you're smiling—"after all, nowadays I cry for no reason at all!").

Dyodyo, my love, why am I writing instead of talking to you? Because I'm uneasy, hesitant to talk about certain things. I've grown touchy, madly suspicious. . . . Your least gesture, one chilly word, wrings my heart, closes my mouth. I can be open with you only in a warm, trusting atmosphere, which is so rare with us nowadays! You see, today I was filled with a strange feeling that the last few days of loneliness and thinking have evoked in me. I had so many thoughts to share with you, but you were in a cheerful mood, distracted, you didn't care

for the "physical," which was all I wanted, you thought. It
hurt terribly, but again you thought I was cross merely because
you were leaving so soon.

Probably, I wouldn't have the nerve to write even now had
you not showed me a little tenderness as you were leaving. It
had the sweet smell of the past and it is the memory of that
past that makes me cry myself to sleep every night. My
dearest, my love, you are impatiently skimming over this letter—"what the hell does she want?" If only I knew what I
want! I want to love you. I want back the tender, serene, perfect time that we both knew. You, my dear, often read me in a
trite way. You always think I'm "cross" because you're leaving
or something like that. For you our relationship is purely superficial, and you cannot imagine how deeply this hurts. No,
no, don't tell me, my dear, that I don't understand, that it is
not superficial, at least not the way I think it is. I know, I understand what it means, I know—because I feel. When you
said such things to me in the past they sounded hollow—now
they are a grave reality. Yes, I feel like an outsider. I feel it
seeing you gloomy, silently brooding over your worries and
problems, your eyes telling me, "This is none of your business,
you mind your own business." I feel it seeing you, after a serious quarrel, reserved, turning over our relationship in your
head, drawing conclusions, making decisions, dealing with me
in one way or another. But I'm left outside and can only spec-
ulate about what's going on in your head. I feel it whenever
we're together, and you push me away, and, locked within
yourself, go back to your work. Finally, I feel it when I think
about my future, my whole life which, like a puppet, is jerked
about by an outside force. My dearest, my love, I don't complain, I don't want anything, I just don't want you to take my
tears as female hysteria. But what do I really know? It is probably my fault, more mine than yours, that our relationship is not
warm, smooth. What can I do? I don't know, I don't know
how to act. I do not know how—I can never plan ahead, draw

conclusions, handle you in a consistent way—I act on the spur of the moment, I throw myself into your arms when bursting with love and sorrow—hurt by your coldness, my soul bleeds and I hate you! I could kill you!

My golden heart, you can understand and reason so well; you've always done it for yourself and for me. Why don't you want to do it now! Why do you leave me alone? Oh, God, how I beg you to come to me, but perhaps it is true—or so it seems to me more and more often—perhaps you don't love me *that much* any more? Truly, truly, I feel it so often.

Now everything I do is wrong. You find fault with me no matter what. You don't seem to have much need to be with me. What makes me think so? I wish I knew. All I know is that, all things considered, you'd be much happier were it not for me. Something tells me you'd rather run away and forget the whole affair. Ah, my dearest, I do understand—I know you don't get much pleasure out of our relationship, with my scenes that wreck your nerves, my tears, with all these trivia, even my doubts about your love. I know, my golden heart, and when I think of it, I'd like to be—hell!—I'd like not to be. It's too painful to think that I invaded your pure, proud, lonely life with my female whims, my unevenness, my helplessness. And what for, damn it, what for? My God, why do I keep harping on it? It is over. My dearest, now you'll ask again, what do I want, finally? Nothing, nothing at all, my dearest. I only want you to know I'm not blind or insensitive to the torment I'm inflicting on you. I want you to know I cry over it, bitterly, but I do not know what to do or how. Sometimes I think it would be better to see as little of you as possible, but then I can't help myself: I want to forget everything and throw myself into your arms and have a good cry. And again this cursed thought creeps in and whispers, leave him alone, he is enduring it all out of kindness. Then one or two trifling episodes prove me right, and my hatred swells. I want to spite you, bite you, show you that I don't need your love, that I can live without it. And I start torturing myself and agonizing, and the vicious circle starts again.

"What a drama!" Isn't it? "What a bore! Same thing over and over again." And I, I feel as though I haven't said one tenth of it and not at all what I wanted to say.

Language is false to the voice,
the voice is false to thoughts;
Thoughts fly up from the soul
before they are caught in words.[2]

Adieu! I almost regret this letter. Perhaps you will be angry? Perhaps you will laugh? Oh, no, do not laugh.

Pray, beloved maiden, welcome the ghost
As in the olden days.[3]

1. L. and J. were never formally married.
2. Adam Mickiewicz (1798-1855), *Dziady,* [*The Forefathers*], part III, a drama, treasure of Polish literary heritage. Incidentally the closing of the play in Warsaw in 1968, because of its allegedly anti-Russian overtones, led to widespread student unrest. (Translated by E. B.)
3. Adam Mickiewicz, ibid., *The Ghost.*

The Trial
1898-1900

In May 1898, in order to work in the center of the socialist movement, Luxemburg moved to Berlin, while Jogiches stayed in Zurich to finish his doctoral dissertation and obtain Swiss citizenship. The decision was not easy. Two years before, she wrote him, "My success and the public recognition I am getting are likely to *poison our relationship* because of your pride and suspicion. The further I go, the worse it will get. That's why I am having second thoughts about moving to Germany. If, after mature consideration, I should come to the conclusion that I have either to withdraw from the movement and live in peace with you in some godforsaken hole, or else move the world but live in torment with you, I would choose the former" (July 12, 1896). "After mature consideration" Luxemburg made the only decision she could make: to stay in the movement *and* with Jogiches.

To secure freedom of action and escape the ever-present fear of deportation, Luxemburg acquired German citizenship (letter 9) through a marriage of convenience. The bridegroom, Gustav Lübeck, son of her Polish-born friend Olympia Lübeck, was not too happy about the arrangement, but no one asked for his opinion. (The divorce proceedings dragged on for years until the marriage was dissolved in 1903.) Equipped with her doctoral degree and the marriage license, Luxemburg set out to storm the bastion of the most powerful socialist organization in Europe, the German Social Democratic Party (SPD).

Within less than six months, with many odds against her as a foreigner, a Jew, and a woman, Luxemburg had made her name in the SPD. She won the respect and support of its leaders Wilhelm Liebknecht, August Bebel, Karl Kautsky, Clara Zetkin, and Franz Mehring. In two years the outsider became a popular contributor to the SPD newspaper, a familiar figure at the SPD party congresses (Stuttgart, Hanover, Mainz) and in the Socialist (Second) International.

Zeal, ambition, and a confirmed sense of her own equality with, if not superiority to, the party authorities made her rebel at the beginning against being sidetracked into the Polish movement (letter 8). Soon, however, she came to personify her cherished idea—internationalism. The leading Marxist expert for Polish and Russian affairs with the German SD party, she was living a double political life. Always active in the Polish and in the German movements, her authority soon extended to the French socialists and to the Russian social democrats. The year 1898 saw her working among the Polish miners in Upper Silesia, publishing the classic "Social Reform or Revolution," an indictment of Bernstein's revision of Marx, becoming editor in chief of *Sächsische Arbeiterzeitung* and participating in the SPD party congress in Stuttgart. In this same year she authored a book, *The Industrial Development of Poland* (letter 7).

Berlin became her permanent residence. Here she moved from one furnished room to another and came to hate them for the rest of her life. "As for our home," she wrote to Jogiches, "I don't even want to think about furnished rooms" (January 22, 1900).

Just as she had predicted, her stunning career did not make her relationship with Jogiches easier. He supported her all the way in word and deed, but her growing fame did not leave him unscathed. A madly ambitious man, he dreaded living in her shadow. While she wanted above all to live with him openly, conspiracy was second nature to him and secrecy a weapon. She was not blind to his ordeal. To placate him, she made constant references to "your doctorate," though he never finished his studies, and assured him "you can write perfectly well," fully aware he could not. Always finding new excuses, he postponed their reunion for two years. She pleaded and threatened, cried in despair, and screamed in anger. Not until he was faced with her ultimatum (letter 32), did he leave his Swiss hideout and join her in Berlin.

Her family in Warsaw, particularly her father, was also a source of constant anguish. It irked her that Jogiches with his penchant for conspiracy insisted on keeping their relationship secret whether it was necessary or not (letters 15 and 17). When, after almost ten years, she finally revealed it to her family, she still had to cheat "like a crook" because of his reluctance to settle down with her. Her mother's death in 1897 left her with a profound and permanent feeling of guilt. Because of "cursed politics," Luxemburg later lamented (letter 66), she had "never had time to answer" her mother's letters and Lina Luxemburg died without seeing her daughter. Now her desperately ill father craved to see her for the last time. Torn between Jogiches, work, and her filial duties, she finally snatched a little time to stay with her father (letter 27). But this belated offering did not assuage her guilt feelings.

In 1898 the Russian Social-Democratic Workers' Party, nine men strong, held its first congress. "Rascals," Luxemburg remarked half jokingly to Jogiches, "and yet they managed" (letter 12). Neither the founders of the party nor anyone else had the premonition that in less than twenty years it would leave the perfectly organized German party far behind and change the face of the world.

Rosa Luxemburg in her Berlin apartment

Leo Jogiches, a commander without troops in Berlin (SPD
Archives, Bonn)

Letter 7

[Berlin]
Tuesday night
[May 17, 1898]

My beloved Dyodyo!

It's the first quiet moment. I'm alone and can write you a long letter. All day yesterday and today I looked for a room with the "cousin" [no relation]. You've no idea how hard it is to find a room in Berlin. [. . .]

Bebel[1] and Auer[2] are here. I haven't written [Bebel] yet because I want to have my own room and look half-decent in case we meet. Incidentally, everybody, or at least my landlady, is impressed with me, and, strangely enough, they think I'm very young and marvel that I already have a doctoral degree. That should calm you down. The Warskis found me "smashing" in my black dress and a new hat. So much for my exterior. My interior is less smashing, though equally black due to Berlin's depressing hugeness. I feel as though I came here all alone, a total stranger, to "conquer" Berlin and am a little scared now that I'm faced with its cold, overwhelming indifference.

I got another piece of paper out of the landlady because I can't part with you. I could go on writing till morning but am afraid you'll take me to task for stuffing too much paper into one envelope. Back to the point. I told you I felt as though my soul were bruised. Let me explain. Last night in bed, in a strange apartment, in a strange city, I indulged myself and deep down toyed with a thought: Wouldn't it be better to end this life on the run and live, just the two of us, in tranquillity and happiness, somewhere in Switzerland, taking advantage of our youth and enjoying each other? Then I looked back and saw emptiness was all I had left behind.[3] And I knew I was toying with an illusion. We had no life together, no joy, no happiness (this refers to our personal relationship not to the

cause—its drawbacks shouldn't interfere with our happiness).
Just the opposite. Looking back at the last six months or more,
all I saw was a tangle of dissonances, incomprehensible,
strange, tormenting, dark. Then the piercing pain in my tem-
ples began and with it an almost physical sensation of bruises
on my soul that wouldn't let me turn right or left. Most tormenting is the confusion, like a dull humming inside my head,
and I don't know any more why, what for, what was it all
about, or was it. . . .

Incredibly, the bruises inspired me with courage, courage to
start a new life. It became clear to me that I had left nothing
good behind, that things would not have been any better had
we stayed together, and I would have gone on living in an atmosphere of constant dissonance, trying to comprehend in
vain and in pain. What I had briefly yearned for was but a fig-
ment of my imagination, and I felt like that cat—remember? in
Weggis—cornered by the dog between the mountain and the
lake. Now, imagine the dog as the life that runs after me; the
mountain as your "rocky heart," faithful and stable like a rock
and like a rock rugged and unapproachable; and finally, the
lake as the waves of life I jumped into in Berlin. Nor is this a
hard choice, between two cudgels, as it were. I must try not to
let myself be swept away by the Berlin waves like that cat. . . .

Since *ça me touche toujours quand je parle de moi-même*, I
feel like having a good cry, but my trained ear instantly hears
your impatient voice, "Stop crying, for heaven's sake, you'll
look like the devil knows what!" Obedient, I put aside the
handkerchief so tomorrow I won't look like the devil knows
what.

And here we go again, don't we! Despite everything you
told me before I left, I keep harping on my worn-out tune,
making claims on personal happiness. Yes, I do have a cursed
longing for happiness and am ready to haggle for my daily
portion with the stubbornness of a mule. But I'm losing it. My
desire gradually subsides in view of the crystal-clear or rather

tomb-dark impossibility of being happy. No happiness without joy, and perhaps our life, that is, our relationship (for me it's one and the same, *vous savez—les femmes* . . .) is joyless and drab. I'm beginning to understand that life can grab one and not let go, and there's nothing one can do about it. I'm just getting used to the idea that my only duty now is to think about the elections and later about what will happen after the elections. I feel like a forty-year-old woman going through the symptoms of menopause, although the two of us together are only about sixty years old.

Naturally after reading this oration, you'll think, "what repulsive egoism, all she can think about is her own 'happiness' regardless of my loss, a hundredfold greater than the loss of a lover's caresses."[4] That's what you'll think, and you'll be wrong. I have not forgotten, not for a second, *your* inner bookkeeping, all in the red. It is constantly on my mind; moreover, on top of my other grudges I bear you a grudge for cutting me off from your bookkeeping and letting me do nothing but keep my mouth shut! As I told you, you are like Rigi, but, alas, I'm no Jungfrau, majestically, in dead silence, staring with her snow-clad top beyond the high skies. I'm just an ordinary kitten who likes to caress and to be caressed, who purrs when happy and meows when unhappy—the only way she can express herself. Since you forbid me to meow, all I can do is write about myself and my boring affairs. But accuse me of egoism, and you miss the mark.

I want the house hunting over, damn it, and I want to get to work, and send you the first "battle cry." I'd be so proud if I pleased you. Unfortunately no business to write about, that's why this letter is so dull.

Do you have any idea how much I love you?

At midnight, before reaching Berlin, the train ran over a man. We were stuck for fifteen minutes, and I woke up to the sound of moaning. It was a peasant with his oxen crossing the

track in darkness. I asked if he was alive, and somebody said,
"*lebt noch a bissele*" [is a little bit alive].

A bad omen.

That's all, my one and only. If you can, write about *yourself,*
write much, much. Your promise to take better care of yourself
made me happier than all your news put together. Write *in de-
tail:* Do you drink cocoa at four? Do you drink milk every
day? Please write about *everything.*

My love, don't be annoyed about the thick paper and the
heavy letter. I haven't unpacked yet.

Keep well, address your letters Kantstr. 55, omit my last
name, put only the first and the patronymic; spies are around
constantly.

Yours

Any news from Anna?

[*Remarks in the margins*]

My room is 1 DM a day.

What's with the dressmaker? I feel guilty about the dress,
should never have ordered it; it cost you a fortune, the dressmaker is unhappy, and I feel terrible about her. Jadzia loves
the hat.

I'm writing home today for a loan.

Have you been to see [Professor] Herkner? Did you start attending lectures? If you knew how much I'd like you to finish;
when I think about your studies, my whole back aches.

Imagine, Mrs. Augsburg is forty years old! She lives now in
Mu[nich] [. . .] and, it seems, is a lady with a "certain past."
The whole literary-artistic Bohemia in Mu[nich] seems to be
reeking with filth. Helena Donninges[5] and her husband, Sze-
wicz, live there too; he's connected with *Simplicissimus.*[6]

Shm[uilov][7] was surprised that my book will be published
by D[uncker] and H[umblot].[8] He said they must have on the

staff an expert on contemporary literature who has heard of
me and that whoever wants to "be a success" tries to get published there.

Daszyński's wife ran away with another man.[9] I understand
her reputation left a lot to be desired, anyway. Daszyński married her, it seems, because the results were already visible. I
hear he's strongly disliked in the party circles in Galicia because he's a rake, amoral, and likes to live like a country
squire.

1. August Bebel (1840-1913), Marxist socialist, with Wilhelm Liebknecht, cofounder and leader of the German Social Democratic
Party (SPD) and its deputy to the Reichstag; one of the central figures in the Socialist International. He was an early fighter for
women's emancipation (*Women and Socialism*, 1883).
2. Ignaz Auer, one of the leaders of the SPD.
3. For an opposite view see letter 23.
4. J.'s mother, Zofia, died in Wilno in 1898.
5. Helene von Dönninges (1843-1911), actress and writer. Ferdi-
nand Lassalle was mortally wounded in a duel over her. Serge
Schewitsch was her third husband.
6. *Simplicissimus*, a famous German satirical weekly.
7. Vladimir Shmuilov-Claassen, a Russian emigrant active in the
SPD.
8. Verlag Duncker & Humblot, well-known publishing house in
Leipzig that published L.'s *The Industrial Development of Poland* in
1898.
9. Ignacy Daszyński (1866-1936), cofounder and leader of the
PPSD (Polish Social Democratic Party), which in 1919 merged
with the PPS (Polish Socialist Party). (See appendix.)

Letter 8

[Berlin]
Saturday
May 28, [18]98

Dyodyu, yesterday I wrote you that I'd just about made up
my mind to go to U[pper] Silesia. I've thought it over again
and again, and I see no other solution.

What I don't like is this:

1. I'd much rather start out "operating" on a bigger stage, like Berlin, than in some godforsaken Silesian hole.

2. At the worst, I'd rather speak in Dortmund—at least there they have public meetings.

3. Since, according to Winter,[1] public meetings can't be arranged in Silesia, my work will be doomed to such obscurity that not even a streetsweeper will know of it.

4. Although I'll act like a governor-general, since I'm totally unfamiliar with the local conditions and work, *de facto* I'll be under Winter's control. There's no way I can gain the upper hand.

5. All in all it is not the éclat we expected.

But:

1. There is no work to be done in Berlin because no one here takes the Poles seriously, and to "devote" myself to the German agitation in Berlin, while leaving the Polish work to Moraw[ski][2] and Winter, would be absurd. The Germans don't give a damn about me, and to cut myself off from the *Polish* work before the elections means to forego the chance of representing the Poles at the party congress. Auer made it abundantly clear to me that for the Germans, Polish agitation means Upper Silesia. *Sapienti sat.*

2. Under the predominant influence of the Germans, Poles in Dortmund pose no threat. Besides, Auer, correctly from *his* point of view, thinks all efforts must be concentrated on U[pper] Silesia. They wouldn't pay for my trip to Dortmund either.

3. To refuse to go to Upper Silesia means rejecting the only Polish election work I was offered, straining my relationship with the executive committee, and appearing a braggart (since I myself requested the work). It also means impairing my relationship with Winter who may eventually emerge as the sole representative of the Polish movement.

4. If I intend to establish an independent position within the

Polish movement, I must set up a direct line of communication with the Silesian workers. Local elections offer the perfect opportunity. This is also important in view of the party congress and obtaining a mandate.

5. Mostly I'd like to spit on both Auer and Winter and proceed on my own, but the question is, where? There's no stepping stone, neither Berlin nor Poznań, and in Upper Silesia I can't do anything alone.

6. In view of the editorship [of *The Workers' Journal*],[3] a good relationship with the executive committee and with Wint[er] is indispensable. Meanwhile, we must lean on the Germans.

So, there's nothing to do but grab my little suitcase and be off. Where to? Probably to Beuthen. I'm waiting for Winter's instructions. I'll write you more before departure. [. . .]

Write soon and about everything.

R.

1. August Winter, founder and leader of the SPD in Upper Silesia (Polish, German-annexed territory), he worked among Polish coal miners.
2. Franciszek Morawski, active in the Polish and German socialist movements and cofounder of the Polish Socialist Party in German-annexed Poland. (See appendix.)
3. Reference to *The Workers' Journal* [*Gazeta Robotnicza*], an organ of the Polish Socialist Party strongly opposed to L.'s idea of an international workers movement and specifically to joining forces with the German and Russian workers.

Letter 9

[Berlin]
Tuesday
[May 31, 1898]

My love! Today (!) at last, after five days, I got both your letters—Friday's and Monday's. Friday's wandered all over Berlin for three days—the postman muffed it. Now, business.

1. Am going to Upper Silesia probably the day after tomorrow; still no news from Winter, so I don't know where to. Am expecting his letter tomorrow but have a good train connection only in the morning. The trip to Król[ewska] Huta (will probably have to drag myself that far) takes twelve hours!! and costs 23 M[arks] for third class and 33 for second. Will travel second class but charge the party for third, so we'll pay the 10 M difference from our own pocket. I'll stop in Wrocław for a day to talk to Br[uhns] and Sz[ebs],¹ as Auer advised me to do. I've already written you about it, I think. Am taking a couple of dresses, underwear, the little cooker in a suitcase borrowed from the cousin.

2. The German lecture is ready, have finished it today. I was itching to give it here before going away but was afraid of Auer and also it would have delayed the trip by three days. Will try to use it at least in Silesia and later, god willing, in Berlin.²

3. Wrote to Parvus.³ Don't have to see him now.

4. Wrote a warm letter to the Seidels.⁴ Władek [Olszewski] wants to go to Galicia for a short time and then move on to Katowice or Sp. near the border to work for us.⁵ I'm trying to convince him to move the central bureau—let's wait and see, will try to have him wait here till I'm back. I'm on very good terms with him; lent him 5 M, poor man is without work. He gave Gut a dressing down for his horseplay.⁶ When I return, he'll introduce me to Chł[osta] and Żaba, and then I'll try to get them in hand.⁷

5. Today got the *Heimatschein* No. 3835, Acta 1979, V H 98 saying, "The undersigned Police Presidium certifies herewith that Rosalia Lübeck, married, born L[uxemburg], on . . . in Zamostz acquired Prussian citizenship through marriage. The certificate is issued for the purpose of travel abroad and is valid for five years only." Date and Winscheid's signature.

I'll take all my documents with me in a separate envelope.

6. As I wrote you, Józio⁸ offered me 130 s[ilver] r[ubles] for

Duncker [to publish the doctoral dissertation], immediately
available, so you don't have to worry. It is a loan, of course,
for one year. They also sent 10 M for me, my poor, dear ones.

7. Will handle Winter as you advise. Am sure we'll see eye
to eye since he seems like a decent fellow, though a Hun.
[. . .]

8. Won't write to Beb[el], it's no use. "Let him know me by
my deeds."

9. *Jour fixe* at the Cl[aassens'] was stuff and nonsense—no
one there but dumbbells.

10. Everything is clear about money, will do fine till the
first, and I thank you!

11. While I'm away, if you want to, you may send the
books and Beethoven to the cousin, who'll keep the house.[9]

12. Wrote to Karol [Lübeck] and to Kaspr[zak],[10] and
mailed them the papers.

13. Paid additional postage for your Friday letter, you little
monkey, 40 pf[ennig]! "Would you please get a supply of thin
paper. . . ."

As always, I read greedily the few personal words at the end
of your letter. Somehow—and I don't know why—they don't
affect me. I can't imagine you being good, gentle, loving, nor
can I imagine myself as the little Chuchya I once was with you
and you clearly still see in me. There's such silence within me,
such cold. I go through the daily routine mechanically, without fear and without fervor, feeling hollow and empty inside.
Naturally, I'm thinking about you constantly or, rather, I don't
think, I feel your constant presence.

Strange—never before was I so totally alone, a foreigner in
the middle of a big city, my tasks heavy, my energy "light"
[in Russian], and with no possibility of asking your advice.
And yet I feel completely indifferent and calm. Somehow
everything's asleep inside me. Only the articles I must write
remain a nagging, distant thought. Will I have the time, the
strength?

Enfin, qui vivra, verra. As you see, I shifted to business—
your style. Perhaps you're right, and in another six months I
will at last turn into your ideal. I hope it won't be the case of
that horse who was trained to eat less and less until one day
he. . . .

You, don't be sad, you, write more about yourself, about
what you are doing. Why do you go to the Seidels so rarely?
It's foolish. And that letter to Wolf?[11] Will it end in talk? You
were to send me the second draft to correct.—I hate the Huns
and Berlin.

Yours R.

Are you still having eggs for breakfast? Or did you give them
up, too? Write! What do you drink at 4 P.M.? How are you
feeling? You badly needed some peace and I hope you will
have it now.

Write to the Warskis!!

1. Julius Bruhns, German social democrat, journalist, active
among Polish miners. Reinhold Schebs (Szebs), former editor in
chief of *Volkswacht.*
2. L. was inconsistent in capitalizing God.
3. Parvus, pseudonym of Alexander Israel Helphand (1864-1924),
Marxist theorist, Russian social democrat, he lived in exile in
Switzerland and Germany. One of the most intriguing and con-
troversial figures in the revolutionary movement, he was allegedly
a go-between in securing Lenin's passage through Germany in
1917.
4. Robert and Mathilda Seidel, friends of L. living in Switzerland.
5. Władysław Olszewski, active in the SDKP; "to move the central
bureau," probably of the Association of Polish Social Democratic
Workers Abroad, from Zurich to Berlin.
6. Stanisław Gut (Gutt), co-leader of the Association of Polish Social Democratic Workers Abroad.
7. Michal Chłosta and Zaba (Frog, pseudonym of Wojciech
Popławski), active in the SDKP.
8. Józef Luxemburg (1868-1936), L.'s youngest brother, a medical
doctor in Warsaw. L.'s other siblings were sister Anna (Andzia),
b. 1858, a teacher of foreign languages; Mikołaj, b. 1860, a mer-

chant; Maksymilian (Munio), b. 1866, an economist; all lived in
Warsaw.
9. Same person L. called cousin in letter 7. No relation.
10. Marcin Kasprzak, a worker, allegedly smuggled L. out of Poland in 1889. He was cofounder and one of the leaders of the Second *Proletariat* (which succeeded the first, so-called 'Great' *Proletariat*), active in the SDKPiL, and a close collaborator of L. He
died on the scaffold in 1905.
11. Julius Wolf, professor of economics at the University of Zurich
and L.'s teacher.

Postcard 10

Legnica
Tuesday morning
[June 14, 1898]

Dyodyu, yesterday's meeting was a great success. I spoke
even better than in Wrocław. Right off the comrades asked me
to stay here for good. They gave me flowers, etc. The police
behaved very decently, didn't even ask me for documents, although on all the street corners big posters announced my
speech.

Today I'm speaking in Goldberg (one hour away from here),
and tomorrow I'll work in the polling office in Królewska
Huta.

That goddamn Winter, I could have created a sensation with
my lecture in Dresden, Leipzig, etc., but it can't be helped,
and we need him. Anyway, the lecture can wait till the elections are over, or perhaps I'll manage to do something with it
during the runoff election. It's too bad though, because I'll
have to write another speech. Bruhns was supposed to give a
talk here, but he got sick and didn't come. I expect to find letters from you in Kr. Huta. Why the devil don't you write about
your citizenship?[1]

Am sending postcards to the Seidels and to the Warskis.

R.

1. In the original here and henceforth "your city council." J. applied for Swiss citizenship in Zurich. L. will return frequently to the subject that J. preferred to pass over in silence because of his reluctance to move to Berlin. Another excuse was earning his doctoral degree (letters 7, 30, 37).

Postcard 11

Legnica
June 15, 1898

Dyodyu, I'm back in Goldberg, waiting for a train to Kr. Huta. It went beautifully in G[oldberg] yesterday. The lecture hall was jammed, and outside there were more people, one on top of the other at the windows. The comrades said they'd never seen such crowds before. I got three cheers right after *Hoch* for the Social Democracy and today, before departure, got a lovely bunch of roses and mignonettes. I'm going back to Kr. Huta and will stay there today and tomorrow. Where to afterward, I don't know. Probably back to Berlin, provided Bruhns doesn't participate in the runoff election. If he does, he won't let me leave, and I prefer to concentrate on one district rather than talk in many different, small places. Anyhow I'll see—perhaps I can work it out and give a talk in Dresden, and I'd prefer that. I expect to find letters from you at Winter's.

K[iss you] on [the] m[outh]
Yours R.

[. . .] Am dead tired. All my money's gone.

Letter 12

[Berlin]
Friday
[June 24, 1898]

My babykins got so angry and scolded me so shamefully.
That much ado just because, ungrateful little pig that I am, I
dared to make a casual remark about your work on the galleys.[1] Frightened, I put all Dyodyo's corrections onto the second galleys, except for the end of the introduction which, in
the hardness of my heart, I left. Seriously that section is indispensable, and I hope you'll forgive me for leaving the only
part in my entire work just as I want it. Let me tell you that
your "lashing" scares me as much as the wagging of a dog's
tail. [. . .]

I wish you'd tell me where to start. I want to tell you a lot
but dread the sheer physical effort—I'm so weak! You're probably displeased with the work I've done or at least not very
pleased. But I am hoping for the best. Not that I'm excited or
enthusiastic, just the opposite. I'm simply calm and optimistic.
You can't imagine how good my first public appearances were
for me. I plunged in, head on, with no idea how it would turn
out. Now I'm convinced that in six months I'll be one of the
best speakers in the party. My voice, my poise, my language—
nothing failed, and, most important, I walked up the platform
without batting an eyelash as if I had done it for the last
twenty years. In two to three weeks the meetings will start
again, and by then I'll come out *avec éclat,* first in Dresden,
then perhaps in Leipzig, finally in Berlin. Don't worry. I wish
everything else were as easy as giving a speech. By "everything else" I mean two things: (1) the article against
Bernstein[2]; (2) the campaign against Morawski [PPS] (*hazer mit
a turkey*). As for the first, you know the difficulties, and that is
where I am counting on your help again. Apropos the Bernstein article, I'd like to start working on it *at once,* therefore (a)

mail *Neue Zeit* regularly, also the back issues for the last two
weeks; (b) the books, that is, Marx. As for (2), the Mor[awski]
campaign, the worst thing is that now, just as in Zurich, I
don't know which side to hit from. It's clear I must take the initiative. The Germans are waiting for me to come up with a
"bombshell." That's what Winter keeps telling me and
Schönl[ank][3]; etc. But what should I do? I've no idea. [. . .]

A break. Just now received your letter and your second corrections of the first three sheets. I almost went into hysterics. I
don't even want to talk about it, it won't help. I'm sending the
sheets off as they are; have just corrected the language. It's a
pity I didn't get the first galleys directly; Humblot's waiting
anyway and he would have waited one more day. In my opinion, some places are now like skimmed milk, one wonders
why they've been left at all. Enough about it. I know you see
things from a different view: over two weeks of insane work, a
lot of wrong figures, etc. I hope we'll never have to do this
kind of work again! I simply loathe this dissertation of mine
just because we invested so much work and effort in it. The
mere thought of it throws me into hysterics. And this is why I
want to tell you the conclusions I've come to concerning our
working methods.

Up to now, our working system has amounted to a waste of
health and energy; it's plain lunacy. Efforts that fail to produce
visible results deserve ridicule not respect. To achieve the
maximum result with minimal effort—that's the right principle.
I've already put it to use. Working peacefully, with ease, without getting upset, without devoting too much time to one issue—that's my system. I wrote my lecture in this manner, and
that's how I'll write the article for *Leipz[iger Volkszeitung]*. In
some cases no amount of work and strain is too much. This
was true for "From Step to Step,"[4] as well as for the article
against Bernstein. In such cases, however, the work is *not*
wasted. It shows in the polish, in the completeness and the
harmony of the form. But to put so much work into the "KP"

article for *Sächsische* [*Arbeiterzeitung*] or into the dissertation is sheer madness. No one will notice, let alone appreciate it. Of course, I'm not thinking about wrong figures that had to be corrected but about a thousand other molehills that, under the microscope of your literary pedantry, grew into mountains. On the whole, when I compare our past efforts with their results, I feel ashamed. That's over. From now on *frisch, froh, frei*—easy joyful work, serious yet brief reflection, what's done is done with, a prompt decision and a prompt execution, and off we go. This is how I've been working without making a single mistake. If I failed to make a public appearance here, the fault is not mine. I was ready and, given the opportunity, I'd have done it well, excellently. But enough boasting, I want to write you about myself, about you, and a million other personal things.

There isn't much I can write about myself. I'd like to repeat what I already wrote, but again you'd misunderstand me and be hurt. "I feel inwardly cold and calm"—you thought I meant it personally, in relation to you, but I was simply complaining about my condition, which still hasn't changed. It's a deadening apathy—I function and think like an automaton, as though somebody else were going through the motions. What is it? Explain it to me. You ask what it is that I lack. *Life,* precisely that! I feel as though something has died inside me. I feel no fear, no pain, no loneliness; I'm just a corpse. It's as if I were an entirely different person from the one in Zurich, and, even in my thoughts, the "I" of that time seems like a different person.

You said in your letter that you're suffering terribly over your mother's death. Perhaps now you'll believe that this is dreadful for me too. It's a pain that neither stops nor passes, not for a single day. In Zurich I noticed that you didn't believe me so I kept my feelings from you, but this dread has been with me both there and here. It comes mostly at night, when I'm in bed, and makes me moan out loud. I don't know about

you, but I don't suffer from the sense of loss or for myself. The
thought that gnaws at me is, What was that life about? What
was it for? Was it *worth living*? I know no other thought as
dreadful as that. It tears me apart. It comes upon me at the
most unexpected moments, odd times. Yesterday I went to see
Professor Eulenburg for my brother. I had to wait a couple of
hours and these thoughts closed in on me. I couldn't keep myself from crying. Luckily nobody saw me (you're probably
nervous about it). I'm writing you about myself, not out of
egoism, but just to show you I do understand what those simple words you wrote me mean ["no one's left at home now"].
I don't know anymore how I came to talk about it.

You ask about my impressions. The only memorable one
I've already mentioned—the cornfields and the Polish countryside. Nothing else remains in my soul. Somehow, I pay no attention to people, I don't notice Berlin. I long for Silesia, for a
small village, I dream of being there with you and got it into
my head that you'd feel just as I do. Wandering through the
cornfields, we'd both start breathing again. You didn't respond—doesn't this idea attract you, don't you believe it is
possible? Which takes me back to our finances: What I have
will carry me over only till the first of the month (perhaps I'll
be left with a few marks) because I'm paying a lot for milk
(one liter a day! and three eggs for supper); also, I spent a lot
on postage. [. . .]

You're mistaken in thinking that Schönlank can barge in on
me any time. He was told no visits without a written note. My
room looks more or less like the one in Zurich minus a bed
and a night table. The washbasin in the corner is hardly no-
ticeable, elegant furniture, a grand piano, and I had the floor
polished in the best Swiss style. Facing the garden is a vine-
overgrown balcony with a small table and chairs. Once the
books and Beethoven arrive, I can safely receive whomever I
please (there's also a hanging lamp and a desk).

Now, small talk. Platter recommended one of my articles in his literature course.[5] (Cousin told me, who heard it from Glasberg.)

Parvus is urging me to come to Dresden (he's starting a revolution again in the newspaper!). I wrote him back that I can't come now, that he should come here (he'll be much more useful to me here, can introduce me to Ledebour, etc.).[6]

Ganelin settled in Berlin, [Rachela] Abramowicz was arrested in Moscow.[7] Oh, I'm bored with these trifles. I'd rather go on about you and me. I can't imagine how you can stand living at the Kohler woman's.[8] I can't stand her, can't even bear the thought of her. Of course, she's altogether different with you.

What do you think about the new Russian "party?"[9] Naturally just what I do; rascals, and yet they managed! But they didn't cause the stir in the papers that they certainly expected. The timing was wrong. *Neue Zeit* will surely follow it up with Akselrod's "undelivered speech" or "unthought thoughts."[10] I subscribe to *Vorw[ärts]*; do you get *Petite Rép[ublique]*? Could you send it to me? I'm starved for a French word.

I meant to ask you what you do all day long, when I remembered those damned galleys. Oh, god, you can't free yourself from my yoke. But that's the end, after this proofreading you'll have time for yourself at last. Surely you stopped going to the university, didn't you? From now on I'm starting on a regular schedule. I took books out of the library (Kuno Fischer and others) and will read regularly every day. Don't forget to send the Gaspey and the Italian grammar. Did you also stop eating because of the galleys? It's really dreadful, you must look like the wrath of god. My dearest love, pull yourself together, eat a *lot* and regularly, will you? My love, let me know that you do!! And take walks! In Zurich you *can* take long walks, but where can I walk? In the stinking streets or in that stupid Tiergarten full of nannies and babies? Luckily, fresh air comes in from my garden. It's getting late, I must go and mail the letter.[11] Write *at once* and say that you're not cross with me any longer, please.

Yours R.

What's the matter with your citizenship?!! Why on earth don't you answer this question?

1. J. proofread and revised L.'s dissertation for publication. After they broke up, he continued to proofread and revise her works (see letter 91).
2. Eduard Bernstein (1850-1932), prominent German socialist theorist. Because of antisocialist legislation, he spent over twenty years in exile, chiefly in England. In 1898 he aroused vehement disputes by his criticism of Marxist theories, denying the inevitability of both a world revolution and an intensification of class struggle.
3. Bruno Schönlank, coeditor of the leading SPD organ *Vorwärts*. From 1894 until his death in 1901, he was editor in chief of *Leipziger Volkszeitung,* the second most important SPD paper in Germany.
4. L.'s article "Von Stufe zu Stufe. Zur Geschiche der Bürgerlichen Klassen in Polen." [Step by Step. The history of the bourgeois classes in Poland.] Published in *Neue Zeit* in 1897.
5. Julius Platter, professor of political science at the University of Zurich.
6. Georg Ledebour, member of the SPD leadership, on the editorial staff of *Vorwärts,* editor in chief of *Sächsische Arbeiterzeitung.*
7. Salomon Ganelin and Rachela Abramowicz, Russian revolutionaries.
8. Mrs. Kohler, J.'s landlady in Zurich.
9. The Russian Social-Democratic Workers' Party held its first congress in Mińsk, in March 1898. A second congress (1903) in Brussels and London split into factions of Bolsheviks and Mensheviks. Lenin led the Russian S. D. Workers' Party (Bolsheviks), and in 1918 he founded the Communist Party of Russia; it was called the All-Union C. P. (Bolsheviks) after 1925, and the Communist Party of the Soviet Union after 1952.
10. Pavel Akselrod (1850-1928), early leader of the Russian Social-Democratic Party, supported Mensheviks. He lived in exile in Switzerland.
11. On September 14, 1899, L. wrote to J., "Don't end every letter with 'I hurry to the post office,' because I'm getting sick of it."

Letter 13

[Berlin]
Monday,
June 27, [18]98

Dyodyushka, my golden, I just received your nasty card full of reproaches. By now you must have my long letter, must know how unfair you were, and that consoles me. But that card ruined my mood, so I had to leave my reading and write you.

Belovedest, how can you be so mean? How can you talk to me like that? Are you out of your mind? You hurt me terribly. But never mind, I'll write because I was going to anyway.

Do you know why it's so hard for me to write to you about what I think and feel? What I said to you in my last letter—that I feel dead—isn't exactly right. The reason came to me yesterday while I was taking a walk. Here it is: the way we have lived our entire life has been influenced by work so much that whether I want it or not, my personal impressions have become almost meaningless to me. My psychological states are unimportant. Indeed, it almost repels me that they exist. I don't want to experience them, let alone write about them. Instinctively all that matters to me are actions and results.

It seems to me, and it's more than possible that I'm wrong, but it does seem that this is all that matters to you, too—everything else is the devil's work. Maybe the deadness I had complained about and really understood only yesterday has been caused by this state of mind; maybe it is simply an abomination of and contempt for all personal emotions and an affirmation of only tangible results. It wouldn't surprise me. After all, our lives have been driven—to the exclusion of everything else—by the desire for and expectation of results, so I could have been easily affected by it.

And there is one more important thing—here, I am without air. If you were here, if we lived together, my life would be normal, and it's possible that I'd like Berlin, and a walk in the Tiergarten could please me. Now, frankly, I've no pleasant experiences. It doesn't make any difference to me whether it rains or shines. I walk the streets without paying the least attention to shop windows or people. At home all I can think of is things to be done, letters to be written, and I go to bed as indifferent as I get up. After all is said and done, the real reason is very simple—you are not here. I feel detached, a stranger to everyone and everything. But again, I'm talking about myself, and I wanted to write about you.

Dyodyuchny, I must admit I was enormously impressed by your last corrections, and I humbly ask your forgiveness for having gotten furious. The fact is you discovered many important mistakes. But it irritates me that you slaved, without eating or sleeping—what a madhouse.

I've already written my article for *Leipzig*[er *Volkszeitung*]. It turned out well—I covered the topic thoroughly and kept a measured tone throughout the whole piece. I haven't sent it off because I still don't have the figures. I didn't send it to you because (1) to copy twelve pages is an awful job; (2) you couldn't get it back to me in time, and I can't delay it any longer because comments about the outcome of the elections shouldn't appear too long after the elections. I hope to get the figures tomorrow; asked Winter for them, and he has already sent word from Austria, where he is on a short vacation, that he would give them to me.

Why won't you answer my repeated question about your citizenship?! If you don't give me a definite answer, I'm going to get rude. I have as many connections here as you have in Zurich, that is, my landlady. I don't know anyone here. I don't feel like calling on the Claassens. It's a bore, and the cousin is just a child busy with her own things, so I'm all by myself all

day long. Yet I enjoy the solitude very much. I don't need any
company but you. You always said I miss people, I just need
somebody around. You can see, can't you, I don't lift a finger
to see anyone. I don't even feel like seeing Fr[au] Ihrer,[1]
though I'll have to, and, much as I don't want to, I suppose I'll
have to see Parvus. I don't feel like talking to anyone or ever
leaving my room. [. . .]

My sister will be coming to visit soon. I don't know if I told
you that Józio's paper won an award (300 s[ilver] r[ubles]) in
the Warsaw Medical Society competition. I was thrilled. He's
also done an article for the *Berliner Mediz. Wochenschrift,*
and that's why I went to see the editor, Eulenburg.

I've a feeling I should go to Leipzig to press Humblot: (1)
concerning the publication of the dissertation in book form (he
didn't answer, and it's awkward for me to write again, particularly since he never stops fuming about the late proofs); (2)
concerning the *Materialien,* etc. But I'm not sure my going
there is necessary, and I really don't have the energy. Maybe I
should go, it's not very expensive. I am concerned with the
book's publication—it would be disastrous if he delayed it till
the fall, and, since the scoundrel keeps referring to the book as
a "dissertation," I should go and get this settled. As for the
Materialien, I can't even mention it in a letter, it's entirely
pointless. Talking in person will make all the difference. To go
or not to go? I'll have to make up my mind by tomorrow, or it
will be too late. I'm scared of the trip, of spending even one
hour on the train.

I feel pretty comfortable in my little room. I've turned everything upside down, and it looks very pleasant, the balcony in
particular. Instinctively I look at everything with your eyes. I
try to guess how you would arrange this, where you would
like that. When will you ever see it?! Write soon!! I kiss you
on the nose and on the mouth.

                                   Yours R.

1. Emma Ihrer organized the socialist women's movement in 1886.
In 1889 she founded the women workers' paper *Die Arbeiterin,*
and then *Die Gleichheit,* later edited by Clara Zetkin.

Letter 14

[Berlin]
July 2, 1898

Dyodyu, you silly, I'm up to my ears in Bernstein, and you
ask "do I love you?" In short, yes, yes, yes. I do love you, yes,
"with a little passion" too. You'll hear from me for that
"little," you just wait. You're lucky you aren't within my
reach.

Thanks for the money, it came today. Paid Auer back right
away. Humblot's silent, obviously printing. Didn't get the
money from Józio yet. Your fears about my [German] language
are absolute nonsense, you find errors in perfectly acceptable
idiomatic expressions. I asked Sch[önlank] to correct my German—wait and see, he won't change a thing.

Tomorrow I'll get my article and will send it to you
at once—you'll like it better when you see it in print.
Sch[önlank] wrote back immediately reminding me *Hamlet*
was stout. I answered briefly, in my former tone, that though I
don't know if he can argue like the Prince, I've no doubt he
equals him in fencing.

Now, most important—Bern[stein]. Although I've a good
idea about the whole article, I don't feel any better because I
also see enormous difficulties. I worked out an excellent outline. There are two difficult problems: (1) to write about crises;
(2) to prove beyond doubt that capitalism must break its neck.
It is *indispensable* to prove it, but this means writing a new,
concise argument for scientific socialism. Help, for heaven's
sake, help! *Speed is* essential because (1) if somebody gets
ahead of us the entire work is wasted; (2) polishing needs
plenty of time. We started out very well. The pieces I wrote in

Zurich are the dough (half-baked, of course) we need—if only I knew *what* to write, the form would take shape then and there, I feel it in my bones. I want it so badly, I'd give half my life for that article. . . .

But mail *Neue Zeit,* for heaven's sake! I've no idea what they're saying! [. . .]

Another request. In Zurich I put away the [Russian] *Financial News,* some torn-out pages with the numbers marked in pencil, all stuff about crises in America and cartels. I've no idea where I put the pile, but I'd like to have it. The issues: [No.] 22, 1897, on the Oil Trust; an article in the same issue about the steel cartel in Austria; No. 42, 1893, about the same Oil Trust; No. 52, 1893, about the crisis in America; No. 13, 1895, on the same. If you find it, take a look at it and send it right away, will you?

Do write to Warski, my dearest treasure, I swear to god, I *cannot.* I didn't go to Leipzig. Parvus and I keep inviting one another, to no avail. I get *Sächs*[*ische Arbeiterzeitung*].

Kiss you on the mouth.
Róża

Would my dearest boy be good and send me my books?! Mommsen too, please.

Letter 15

[Berlin]
July 10, 1898

Dyodyurochka, my golden! I've a dreadful migraine, my throat feels choked, I can hardly write and will be brief! Your last postcard hit me hard—all of a sudden a jarring sound broke the harmony! I was sure my little gift would really please you, if only as a token of my deep *desire* to please you. But here we are! Though I loved and caressed you in those

fragmentary, shapeless letters, though I thought about you and
sent you proof, though by sheer luck it arrived on your birthday—no good![1] "The form"—that's what counts! Formal birthday wishes; only *that* matters! Poor me, I thought you'd get it
on the nineteenth [Jogiches's birthday was on the eighteenth].
What priggishness, what an odd misinterpretation of another
person's feelings, what a disgusting tone! You probably think
your saying "you know I don't like presents" is immensely
clever, but it is very silly. When will I change you for the better, when will I tear this damn anger out of you?

Apropos, it was very tactless to send me back unread the
letters of my "friends," Sch[önlank] and Br[uhns], with the
comment "too long to read." Obviously in this case, too, you
thought you had made *un très beau geste* but let me tell you,
you behaved crudely. Here I *wanted* to share these letters with
you, to discuss these people in a purely personal way, and to
share my impressions with you. You shouldn't have reacted
like a "noble husband" straight out of a novel who magnani-
mously returns to his wife the letters of her admirers, unread,
to prove he is beyond good and evil. But in our own usual,
straightforward way, you should have read these letters,
thought them over, and written me your impressions. Why did
this occur to me? Because they both, particularly Sch[önlank],
write me long, interesting letters every other day. But there's
no one to share my thoughts with. Let me just tell you what
being a German means! In his last letter, without mincing
words, Br[uhns] wrote that he has gone to the dogs because of
his wife. Were he under my influence, says he, he'd have
amounted to something. And this from a man who's almost
forty! They are a species entirely different from us.
Sch[önlank], on the other hand, is very sophisticated and well
educated. Our correspondence follows the tone set by me,
part scholarship, part salon: we discuss Kant and other things
(which neither of us ever read, as you hasten to add, you
wicked one).

You got your just desserts, you feel ashamed and disgraced in my eyes. Good. Now let's get to more serious matters. Humblot sent you the dissertation. Take it to Ruegger, order the diploma, I'll send you the money. H[umblot's] bill amounts to 162.50 and 33 for revisions. Modest, isn't it? He even apologized for the excessive bill. I'm sending you two out of the seventeen copies of the book and separately one to Seidel. It looks pretty, doesn't it? You'll poke fun at me, but I have to admit my heart quivered, and I blushed as I was opening the package. Oh, my head's killing me.

I'm working bravely nowadays. Arranged things with Parvus most successfully; am writing short pieces for him, like those you have, about Poland, France, and Belgium. They reimbursed my magazine subscription—30 M quarterly! Of course, it's in addition to the fee. Tomorrow I'll take out subscriptions to P[etite] Ré[publique] and Peuple. It takes me one hour to write one piece, and I plan to read the newspapers and write regularly at a fixed hour in the morning. I write fast, make a fair copy, and send it off (it would give you an apoplectic fit three times a day). There'll be *Geld* at the end of the month! And Parvus is happy. Needless to say, he showers me with requests, "why not at the same time England and Italy and Turkey," but I only laugh and don't bother to answer.

Something profitable (and permanent) may also turn out with *Leipziger* [*Volkszeitung*]. I worked on it for the last three days (that's why I was too busy to write you). I'll write you more when I hear from them, in a few days. See! Throw a tantrum! . . . Nights I work on the Bernstein article, hell and damnation, what a difficult thing. Oh, my head's splitting. Let me know to whom else I should send the book. I'm sending you the galleys, you're boring the hell out of me. And stop threatening me with a boycott, will you? Just wait! I'll cure you of all these [illegible word].

But I haven't mailed you the Webbs yet. Today received *Neue Zeit*. Sent Auer 54 M. My sister's coming in a few days, perhaps also Józio with his wife and child (he had been invited to a convention of Polish physicians in Poznań and, as the prize-winner, to deliver a lecture but, as you probably know from the papers, "foreigners" were not admitted, and the convention broke up over this issue). I'll do what you want, and I won't enlighten my family about us. My sister is bringing me a dress again. Oh, my head. I understand from your postcard you're working on your dissertation. Am I right? Cheer me up, tell me everything about it. The topic? etc. How is it going with [Professor] Herkner? You know, that idiot [Professor] Wolf nagged me to write something for him when I saw him last. He has shed all the wisdom we crammed into him and is as stupid as ever. He could use another course with you.

Did you write to Warski? I didn't, not a word. I know I'm a pig but I can't, not for the life of me. I must stop, my headache makes me nauseous.

I want to know whether you have repented after this letter; write at once.

> I don't kiss you on the nose
> or on anything else.
> R.

---

1. Many years later, in 1916, L. wrote to Luise Kautsky in connection with another gift she gave J., ". . . I sent a wonderful picture from the [Turner] collection to Leo . . . and got back a message. . .: declined with thanks—this would amount to 'vandalism'—the picture must be returned to the collection! Genuine Leo, isn't it! . . . he does not know 'how to love. . . .'" Rosa Luxemburg, *Briefe an Karl und Luise Kautsky,* Luise Kautsky, ed. (Berlin: E. Laub'sche Verlagsbuchhandlung GmbH, 1923), p. 193.

Postcard 16

[Berlin]
[August 22, 1898]

My dearest, my beloved, my nice and kind one! I haven't answered your scolding!—I'm weak and can't get angry. Now you're being good, but I'll never forgive you for having been angry, because I'm sure you'll be angry again when we live together even for a week. I asked my heart several times—but, no, I can't forgive you, I'm unable to revenge myself, and I cannot forget.

I'm terribly weak, partly for the usual physical reason—only your presence could make me feel better. But I'm pulling myself together and slowly recovering. I don't know why, but I can't put on paper all I'd like to tell you, there is so much of it. I'm a very serious person now and have been thinking a lot about your life and mine. I'm so weak that the pen slips out of my fingers. I'm barely alive after writing a card to you and must save the rest of my strength to work on Bern[stein]. Yesterday I finished the first draft and now am trying to polish it. Am reading the Webbs and found some material there. Seems to me with more hard work something outstanding may emerge even from this draft. But I must keep working and re-working it. To write an outline and a summary for you is a nuisance and pointless to boot. I'd like to put it into decent shape quickly and send you the entire thing. I know you'll pick up the main thread immediately and add the finishing touches. After all, the more I have to rely on myself the better. I'm ashamed to wear laurels that are rightfully yours in front of the whole world, but your help with my finished work remains within the bounds of decency.

Winter sent me *Katt[owitzer Zeitung]*. *Eve[ryman's] Journal* reprinted from Lwów's *Pol[ish] Word*. There was a paragraph in *The Voice*—soon they'll publish a long review.[1]

Kiss you!

1. Reviews and notes following the publication of L.'s *The Indus-trial Development of Poland*. *Everyman's Journal* is *Dziennik dla Wszystkich; Polish Word* is *Słowo Polskie; The Voice* is *Głos*.

Letter 17

My dear Dyodyu! I'm writing in bed, or rather lying on the sofa, unable to get up, unable to eat, not even a bite, for the fifth day in a row. Today I feel slightly better, can drink tea with milk, and hope I will get better soon. I don't have to tell you that I'm furious my work has been interrupted. Szirman comes every day to "treat" me, that is, she brings medicine (which I pretend to take).[1]

Though it's hard for me to write, I want to take advantage of the "free" time and write you a long letter. I received the money, and will save 40 M or spend it on a jacket and shoes, if you can spare it for that.

First, about our getting together. How you ever figured out that if I can come and stay with you now, "I could have done it as well a month ago" is a puzzle. Just as before, I cannot come "now," that is, at once, because of my daddy. Now, just as before, I cannot refuse to see him. If you could come here in two weeks as I have suggested, I could, in the *mean-while,* see daddy (anyhow, you wouldn't be ready earlier be-cause of those affairs of yours which, by the way, I don't un-derstand). I can't arrange things with daddy just like that, my precious, because he too is busy. Besides, he never answered my last letter in which I said his visit must be postponed by a few weeks (on the one hand thinking of my work, on the other hoping you would come here). Is he cross or something, I've no idea—I'll write again tomorrow.

You can't even imagine the problems all this creates for me. Just a short time ago Józio was here with his wife. Imagine

what would have happened if they had not found me here!
And how will it look if they don't find me here on their way
back? I must keep up some appearances to make them accept
my way of life. First, when daddy wanted me to invite him
right away, I happened to be very busy. Then, when Józio
wanted me to go to Wiesbaden for a vacation with him, I happened, for a change, to be unable to take any vacation. And
all of a sudden I'm off to Switzerland for a vacation! What will
they think?! I must arrange my trip so that they don't find out
about it. That's why I must *wait* till Józio comes here on his
way back, which will be in another three weeks. To you, of
course, all this seems like nothing, but I *can't* ignore them altogether precisely because they don't *interfere* with anything I
do (none of them ever dared to ask how I obtained my German residence permit!).

See, everything would have been fine had you come here.
And don't you pull my leg with tales about "string-pulling"
with the municipal authorities. What that amounts to I well
know from Weggis. You wouldn't need any documents here—
we would be absolutely free—that's what I wrote and that's a
fact, and you didn't have to strain your brain and try to know
everything better than I. Now it turns out that you also have
some Munich documents, so what's the problem? And what's
the "string-pulling" about? *Mais c'est drôle, mon cher,* you've
pulled as many strings there as I have here.

Even now I can't go away for a longer time. How I will get
the newspapers, write the articles, goodness only knows, and
besides, in a month business will start in earnest, and I should
be right *here*. But it doesn't matter anymore, since I've got to
be near Stutt[gart] during the party congress, so it makes more
sense for me to go there than for you to come here. But I repeat, I can't arrange it sooner than in about three weeks. If
you want, you can come here at once, but then what about
Stutt[gart]? I've no idea. I may go there for nothing, perhaps
the discussion won't even start, but not to go is risky!

I don't insist that we meet in Munich. I thought *you'd* like
that best (concerts, galleries, etc.). I don't understand why you
keep avoiding the Warskis. To go on pretending about our relationship in front of them is more than an exaggeration; it is
simply hypocritical. As to their company, I for one was looking forward to seeing them. You know I like nothing better
than going to see people with you or having them come to us.
There's no problem with the Shmuilovs as they live outside the
city in the country. But, as I told you, I don't insist on Munich.
Honestly, I'm in no mood for the country. It's only your imagination that you need the *countryside* for your health and
nerves. Here in Berlin I've become convinced ten times over
that this is a lot of nonsense. In that stuffy city, within a few
weeks I regained my health and my balance, whereas in Weggis I lost weight regularly and was wasting away, and so were
you. Good health depends on the way one lives and on inner
peace, not on the country or the city. Furthermore, fall is coming on, rainy and chilly, a wretched time to be in the country.
Still, the decision is up to you. I've only one reservation: my
dear, let it be any place but Switzerland! It wrecks my nerves
to change constantly from one kind of atmosphere to another,
and besides, Switzerland is associated in my mind with a hollow, bewildering sensation. I'd rather go back there under entirely different circumstances. Why don't you pick out a place
in Bavaria or Swabia?

Now, business. Why should you request *Sozialistische
Monatshefte!* Strange. Don't you ever go to *Leseverein* [Read-
ing Union]? They're there. I'll send them anyway when I get
well. I don't have *Kölnische Zeitung* myself, and as long as I'm
in bed I can't get it. I asked Schönlank which issue the review
[of Luxemburg's book] had been published in but he forgot to
tell me. As for your advice that I should "guide his pen," it's
absolutely out of the question. It's not a matter of standing on
ceremony but of what's proper and when. With Schönlank, it's

not proper, I'd only discredit myself in his eyes *for nothing.* He's impervious in business, the beast. But I hope his review will be favorable to us since he is shrewd, knows what I want, and shares our viewpoint. Anyway, he told me *post festum* that he had written the review and would have it published shortly.

As for Jaurès,[2] I had Urbach[3] take the initiative, because he badly wants to finagle Jaurès into writing an editorial on the Polish question in connection with my book. I, too, will egg him on but not now because, first, Jaurès is out of Paris, and, second, all hell broke loose over the Dreyfus affair and nothing else matters. When the storm blows over, I'll prod Urbach to fix Jaurès. Meanwhile, I keep writing Urbach lest he cools off.

I certainly don't like your telling me not to buy a jacket without you, because I'll buy "the devil knows what." That's just what I don't want you to do, to keep meddling in such womanish stuff. If I'm independent enough to perform single-handed on the political scene, that independence must extend to buying a jacket. I don't have such a poor opinion of my taste; rather, I feel quite confident about it. Well, have you been told what's what?

Your brother can come to Bavaria or Swabia, can't he?— Urbach will send me *Devenir S[ocial]*. I don't get *Le Socialiste*, but that's trash, never even mentioned anywhere, never carrying timely articles.

I'll take my seminar paper with me. You won't scold me anymore, will you? I must stop, blood's rushing to my head. I think I answered all your questions.

I kiss you tenderly.

Yours R.

1. Szirman, a Russian woman revolutionary living in Berlin.
2. Jean Jaurès (1859-1914), professor of philosophy, leader of French socialists and of the Socialist International; founder of the

newspaper *L'Humanité* in 1904. He was assassinated by a nationalist on July 31, 1914.
3. Ignacy Urbach, a Polish socialist living in exile.

Postcard 18

[Berlin]
[September 6, 1898]

Dyodyonnu dear! I wanted to write you a long letter today, but Władek Ol[szewski] just came and is leaving tomorrow for Munich (he was expelled from Prussia while in Wrocław). Naturally I want to spend as much time as I can with the poor man.

Of course, I'll come to Zurich, nothing really matters, I'd be happy with you anywhere.

Gut is corresponding with Heinrich! Mailed you *Sozialistische Monatshefte* and *D[evenir] Soc[ial]* today.

I embrace you.
Yours R.

Letter 19

[Berlin]
September 10, [1898]

My golden darling, last night I received your letter. It's fine you have two sponsors (*curiosum!* Seidel had written me about his good deed *before* he did anything!). Your plan to come *here now* seems worse than my coming to Zurich. Józio and his family will charge in any day now and may stay for a whole week (she'll get a nanny for the child so she can do some shopping). Since they hang around my place all day long, you'll have to vanish into thin air. Worse yet, they want the room next to mine, where they stayed before. That's the room I wanted to put you up in—the only possibility for us to have some privacy.

Even if I put you up in this room, and you disappear when they come, I still can't gag my landlady. You can imagine what would happen if she mentioned you to them. (N.B. They keep needling me about my not getting married—afraid, I suppose, that I'm somehow committed. They do drop hints about *you*.) Now, if you come here before they do, they're bound to find out, and when you disappear they'll jump to all kinds of shoddy conclusions. The week they visit is *lost* for us, mind you, so you see, don't you, that we've nothing to gain by *rushing* our meeting.

Of course, I'd be happy to have you in *my home* instead of being your guest. Of course, I'd like you to see how I live, and I'd like you to see everything yourself. Besides, I'm really scared of the train trip, but I'd rather do that than have you live in hiding. One more thing: no matter where you stay, it would be absolutely impossible to hide your daily visits from my landlady's daughter. The girl is going [to Warsaw] as a nanny with my family, she knows my sister well, and surely you understand that I cannot possibly ask her not to mention you to my sister. Darn it! Our plans for the summer together remind me of that love affair in the *Gartenlaube: Träume sind Schäume oder stille Liebe mit Hindernissen* [*Dreams are Mere Shadows or Secret Love with Obstacles*].

I plan to stay with you even longer than a month. I count on spending lots of time working with you on two speeches so that I can take them back and won't lose time on them here. Meanwhile, you won't miss the beginning of the term. My dislike of Zurich mustn't bother you. We'll be together the whole time, so why should I care about Zurich. What could be nicer than walking up the Zurichberg with you every day. Write *at once* and tell me definitely what you have decided.

You said in your letter that the baron "should be taught a lesson."[1] But *how?* I sent you *D[evenir] S[ocial]* for no other reason but to have *you* tell me how! And send it back, because I must return it to poor Urbach; it's not his copy (I'll copy those two pages). They [PPS] were certainly impressed by the article, weren't they? Clearly, it makes their blood boil that I wrote it. I'm sending you the last issue of *The Workers' Journal*. It's the first attack on me since I've come to Germany. For god's sake, tell me: What should I do about those filthy pigs? Write *to them*—it's wasting one's breath! Write to *Vorwärts*? I can't have it out with them in *Vorwärts* either. Second, it makes me sick to start another third-rate brawl, and finally, will they publish it? I could turn to the executive committee, but I feel like doing it as much as swallowing castor oil. There now, write quickly. What shall I do?

Leipziger Volkszeitung asked me to write a review of Issaeff's *Finanzministerium* and has already sent me a copy. Seems I'll have to accept (Schönlank pressed me several times for an article). He still hasn't published the review of my book. I got *Kölnische Zeitung* and am mailing it to you. It's drivel. Sch[önlank] couldn't have had this paper in mind, or he made a mistake—I'll ask him. I'm feeling better, have been going out for the last three days. The landlady's daughter is an excellent nurse, and I'll soon be all right.

> I embrace you warmly and
> *am waiting for your response.*
> Rózia.

1. Kazimierz Kelles-Krauz, sociologist and philosopher, prominent member of the Polish Socialist Party (PPS).

Postcard 20

[Berlin]
[September 25, 1898]

I've just come back from Dresden again and wired you, my golden one, that I had accepted the editorship.[1] I'm swamped

with work and can't even dream about writing a longer letter.
Tomorrow I must see Mehring,[2] Stadthagen,[3] Schippel,[4] etc., to
solicit articles from them. They'll write for me, or I'll take them
by the scruff of the neck. If I can manage, I'll go back to Dresden this week to hold an open meeting and introduce myself to the masses. At the same time I have to prepare two
speeches for Stuttgart and perhaps drop by the editorial offices
the day after tomorrow. My articles in *Leipziger Volkszeitung*
are a tremendous success. Parvus wanted to wire his congratulations, and Clara Zetkin wrote a letter to Schönlank, a song of
praise about "the valiant Rosa who pummels that flour-sack
Bernstein so vigorously that clouds of powder rise into the air.
And the wigs of the Bernstein school fly off because nothing is
left to powder them with!"[5] These articles have influenced the
decision of the press commission (seventeen members) which
elected me *unanimously*. Kaden shouted, What? Petticoat politics?[6] But they laughed in his face and later on he himself said
to me, "Yes, your articles on the Eastern question were excellent." Jaurès, when he received my book, said, *"Ah, c'est de
Rosa Luxemburg!"* and immediately put it in his pocket. Urbach had talked to him and Jaurès *promised* to write the article as soon as he has a free moment. I'll write to him from
Dresden to ask for an article on the Dreyfus affair for *Sächsische Arbeiterzeitung*. I'll have Seidel work on the Swiss affairs. In a hurry! My belovedest!

                                                    Yours R.

1. L. was editor in chief of *Sächsische Arbeiterzeitung* until November 1898. She accepted the job over J.'s categorical objection who,
when told about the offer, cabled her from Zurich, *"rundweg
ablehnen"* [unconditionally decline]. She resigned over an editorial
policy issue and was replaced by G. Ledebour.
2. Franz Mehring (1845–1919), prominent historian, biographer of
Marx, left-wing social democrat, cofounder of the German Communist Party, one of L.'s closest collaborators. After her falling
out with Kautsky in 1910, Mehring supported her extreme leftist

policy, which culminated in the foundation of the *Spartakusbund,* the predecessor of the KPD (1918).

3. Arthur Stadthagen, lawyer, on the editorial staff of *Vorwärts,* SPD deputy to the Reichstag.

4. Max Schippel, editor of the SPD weekly *Der Sozialdemokrat.*

5. Clara Zetkin (1857–1933), editor of the SPD women's paper *Die Gleichheit,* founding member of the German Communist Party. She was the author of "Lenin on the Woman Question," of several works on socialism and women's rights, and a communist member of the Reichstag from 1919–1932. She was a close personal friend of L.

6. A. W. Kaden, leading figure in the Dresden SPD.

Letter 21

[Berlin]
December 3 [1898]

Yesterday I was at Mehring's and came home sadly convinced there's nothing for me to do but sit down and write "a great work." Mehring, just like Kautsky, asked me at once, "Are you working on a major opus?"[1] The question was put so seriously that I felt I "need" to create this opus. Well, obviously I look like a person destined to write a great work, and there's nothing I can do but prove the general expectation true. Any chance you have an idea what that great work is?

My golden one, if you dispense with that report about my visit with Bebel and Kautsky, I'll return the favor with a faithful account of my conversation with Mehring; it's much more interesting. Well, first, he repeated several times I had done an excellent job editing *Sächsische Arbeiterzeitung,* much better than Parvus, "one saw the paper was actually edited," and that under my editorship the paper was at its best. He said this to Kautsky, too.

2. Both he and his wife (and, I suppose other oldtimers) consider Ledebour only a temporary substitute for me and are convinced I'll go back to Dresden and then exercise my dicta-

torship. They're funny; I'm amazed that they take my return
for granted.

3. When Bernstein was mentioned, Mehring said to me,
"You gave him a sound thrashing in *Leipziger Volkszeitung*. I
was very pleased."

4. Neither Mehring nor the others believe Schönlank's radi-
calism can last, and they asked me what had made him support us in Stuttgart.

Mehring is convinced Ledebour won't last in Dresden much
beyond Christmas because first, he is so outrageously lazy that
any day now he'll show up in his office at noon; second, he is
so cantankerous he can't work with anyone longer than a few
weeks; third, as a theoretician he is an ignoramus with no idea
how to run a paper. M[ehring] knows him well because they
worked together on *Volksblatt*.

5. At one point, the conversation touched on Mehring's re-
fusal to contribute to *Sächsische Arbeiterzeitung*. I told him
frankly what I thought of it. He assured me sincerely that he
simply couldn't work for three papers at once. Had he known
that I didn't want regular contributions but an expression of his
solidarity, he would have written some articles. He'd certainly
contribute, he said, if I took over the editorship again. I suppose that's all, except that we discussed *de omnibus res* of the
party, and we parted on very friendly terms.

The interesting news I promised you is that for several
weeks the police have been watching me. The last few days,
day and night, two undercover agents hung around the
janitor's place and followed me step by step. The janitor, a
former comrade, kept me secretly informed. Then I got fed up
and went straight to the police, to Mr. Lieutenant, and put my
cards on the table. I said that if this did not stop, I'd go to
Windheim [the police chief of Berlin] and raise hell. Of
course, Mr. Lieutenant pretended total ignorance, but the next
day the agents were gone. Mehring advised me, in case they
show up again, to put a paragraph in *Vorwärts* and they'd dis-

appear into the woodwork. What the hell's going on? I've an idea it's a case of mistaken identity. Either they take me for somebody else or somebody else for me. In any case, I'm on my guard, I burned letters, registered myself, went through papers. Most probably this'll be the end of it. [. . .]

Yesterday I got the money, 80 M, and hope to god it's the last time I have to take money from you. [. . .]

Physically I'm still very weak, and though I am taking good care of myself, I could sleep twenty hours a day.

Write about yourself, a lot. [. . .]

A thousand kisses, yours R.

Once I start writing, I'll send you the details so that you can help me.

1. Karl Johann Kautsky (1854-1938), prominent German-Austrian socialist and Marxist, dominant theoretician, leading figure in the Socialist International, cofounder of the Independent Social Democratic Party in Germany in 1917. He was an opponent of Bernstein and later of Lenin and Bolshevism. His friendship with L. (essential, like that of A. Bebel, in establishing her position in the SPD) ended by 1910 when L. charged the SPD with betraying "class interests" for the sake of political expediency. She remained a close friend of Kautsky's wife, Luise, despite her initial apprehension (see letter 38).

Letter 22

[Berlin]
Sunday
[January 22, 1899]

My dear Dyodyu! I waited and waited for the letter you had promised, but when I got the short one I didn't feel like writing for several days, and even now it's hard to write. As I told you many times in Zurich, I find your whole attitude toward the Russian revolution horrendous and disgusting. Eventually

one has to face up to the fact that it is senseless to sit back
idly and just gripe and criticize. I never liked the way you
kicked every Russian who tried to get near you. One may boycott or "punish" some people, a group, but not a *whole
movement*! Your behavior is unbecoming to a strong, high-
minded person—it fits an "embittered all-time loser" like Krichevsky. I'm not telling you all this because of your comments
concerning *my* intended involvement with the Russian revolution, which leaves me entirely cold. I disagree with your
views, but this is too trivial to argue about. Personally *I* don't
give a fig about the whole Russian revolution. I thought that
those connections might be useful to *you*. Of course, only if
you *want* to get involved. Your complaints that they don't
come to *you* are simply ridiculous, as you certainly knew
when you wrote to me. Everybody who turned to you got
the same treatment on principle: mockery, "spitting and
slapping," as you yourself put it. How can you expect them to
come to you?

As for their assumptions that you and I have broken off,
you're absolutely wrong because I've talked about you with
Szirman and others to make our relationship clear, so that all
of them are perfectly aware of it. (For instance, Sz[irman]
knows you stayed with me in Dresden.)

As for saving Szirman "from this milieu," if you'll pardon
me, my "enlightening" her before I can give her something
better to do will amount to nothing but dragging her away
from the revolution. It's better for her to do something, however insignificant and trivial, than do nothing but ridicule others. This kind of entertainment one should reserve for *oneself,*
but one mustn't entice others. Also you seem to forget that
"what makes a German thrive makes a Russian croak." You
know why you make fun of *Soyuz* [Union of Russian Social-
Democrats Abroad], but when characters like Szirman or Fir-
yukov do the same, they go downhill in no time. That's why
I'm very reluctant to let such cubs in on what's going on be-

hind the scenes, particularly when, as I already said, I'm unable to offer them anything better.

Forgive me for writing all this. Perhaps it'll hurt, even anger
you, but for once I, too, must tell you the truth. Think it over,
and you'll have to admit that I'm right. The stand you've
taken, and have been stubbornly clinging to for years, is simply *beneath* your dignity. It's *unworthy* of a man of your stature. Just to spite them, I'd *praise* everything they do rather
than sit back and criticize. Let me repeat, so that there's no
misunderstanding between us: I'm telling you all this *not* to
justify *my* participation in this whole "revolution," which I
don't give a hoot for, but only because of your attitude toward
this "revolution." [. . .]

Why haven't I heard from you?! Don't wait for my letters
and write often, whenever you feel like it. I'm waiting for your
letters!!

> I embrace and kiss you
> warmly.
> Yours R.

[. . .]

Letter 23

[Berlin]
March 6 [1899]

My dear, beloved Dyodyo! A thousand kisses for your
dearest letter and the birthday present, even though it hasn't
come yet.[1] This year presents rain on me. It's a real horn of
plenty. Just imagine—a fourteen volume, deluxe edition of
Goethe from the Schönlanks. With your books it makes a
whole library. My landlady will have to give me another book-
shelf. You can't imagine how happy your present made me.
Rodbertus is my *favorite* economist. I can read him over and
over again for sheer intellectual pleasure. I feel it's not a book

I got but an *estate,* a house, or a piece of land. As soon as all
our books are here, we'll have an impressive library, and
when we finally settle down together we must buy a glass-
enclosed bookcase.

My golden, my dearest, how you delighted me with your
letter. I kept reading and rereading it from beginning to end.
At least six times. So, you are really pleased with me! You
write that maybe, deep down, I know there is a man named
Dyodyo who belongs to me! And you, don't you know that
everything I do is with *you* in mind. Always. When I write an
article, my first thought is you'll be thrilled by it. And on days
when I doubt my strength and can't work, one thought nags
me, how will it affect you? Will I be letting you down? Disap-
pointing you? Proof of success, like this letter from Kautsky, I
see only as moral support for *you.* I *give you my word,* cross
my heart, that I *myself* don't care about Kautsky's letter. I was
ecstatic about it because I read it with your eyes and felt your
pleasure. So I'm waiting impatiently for your response. (It will
probably come tomorrow with the books, a double pleasure.)

I only need one thing for my inner peace, to see *your* life
and our relationship settled. Soon I'll have such a strong moral
position here that we'll be able to live quietly together,
openly, as husband and wife! I'm sure you understand it yourself. I'm happy your citizenship is at last almost settled and
your doctorate near completion.[2] In your last letters I sensed
your excellent mood for work. In fact, during the Schippel
campaign your letters stimulated my thinking day by day, and
in your last letter you gave me an entire piece for my article,
which stands out like a jewel—the piece about the effects of
the "relief" on workers I translated word for word from your
letter.[3]

Don't you know I see and appreciate that at the "sound
of a trumpet" you are at my side at once, helpful, encouraging me to work, the scoldings and my "negligence" all
forgotten! . . . You can hardly imagine with what joy and im-

patience I wait for every letter from you. I know that each will
bring me strength and joy, support and encouragement to go
on.

I felt happiest about the part of your letter in which you
wrote that we are both still young and able to arrange our personal life. Oh, Dyodyo, my golden one, if only you keep your
promise! . . . Our own small apartment, our own nice furniture, our own library; quiet and regular work, walks together,
an opera from time to time, a small, *very* small, circle of
friends who can sometimes be invited for dinner; every year a
summer vacation in the country, one month with absolutely
no work! . . . And perhaps even a little, a very little baby? Will
this never be allowed? Never? Dyodyo, do you know what
possessed me all of a sudden during a walk in Tiergarten?
Without exaggeration! All of a sudden, a little child got under
my feet, three or four years old, blond, in a pretty little dress,
and staring at me. A compulsion swelled in me to kidnap the
child, to dash home and keep it for my own. Oh, Dyodyo,
won't I ever have my own baby?

And we will never fight at home, will we? Our home must
be quiet and peaceful, like everybody else's. But, you know,
what does worry me—somehow I feel so old and homely. You
won't have a handsome wife to take out for a walk in Tiergarten. We'll keep away from the Germans. Despite Kautsky's invitations, I'll keep to myself, let *them* curry my favors, and let
them see how little I care.

Dyodyo, if only you'd settle your citizenship, finish your
doctorate, live with me openly in our own home. We will
both work and our life will be *perfect*!! No couple on earth
has the chance we have. With just a little goodwill we will be
happy, we must. Weren't we happy when just the two of us
lived and worked together for long stretches of time? Remember Weggis? Melide? Bougy? Blonay? Remember, when we are
alone, in harmony, we can do without the whole world?
More, I'm afraid of the least intrusion. Remember, last time in

Weggis, when I was writing "Step by Step" (I always think
with pride about that little masterpiece!), I was sick, writing in
bed, all upset, and you were so gentle, so good, sweet. You
soothed me, saying in that warm voice of yours that I still
hear, "Now, now, calm down, *everything will be fine.*" I will
never forget it.[4] Or, do you remember, the afternoons at
Melide, after lunch, when you sat on the porch, drinking black
thick coffee, sweating in the scorching sun, and I trudged
down to the garden with my "Administrative Theory" notes.
Or, do you remember, how once a band of musicians came
on a Sunday to the garden, and they wouldn't let us sit in
peace, and we went on foot to Maroggia and came back on
foot, and the moon was rising over San Salvadore, and we had
just been talking about my going to Germany. We stopped,
held each other on the road in the darkness and looked at the
crescent moon over the mountains. Do you remember? I still
smell that night's air. Or, do you remember, how you used to
come back from Lugano at 8:20 at night, with the groceries—I
ran downstairs with a lamp, and we carried the bags upstairs
together—then I unpacked them and put the oranges, the
cheeses, salami, the cake on the table. Oh, you know, we
have probably never had such magnificent dinners as those,
on the little table in that bare room, the door to the porch
open, the fragrance of the garden sweeping in, and you, with
great finesse, scrambling eggs in a pan. And from afar in the
darkness the train to Milan was flying over the bridge, thundering. . . .

   Oh, Dyodyo, Dyodyo! Hurry up, come here; we'll hide
from the whole world; the two of us in two little rooms, we'll
work alone, cook alone, and we'll have a good, such a good
life! . . . Remember, you said, "there are no other hands like
yours, delicate hands."

   Dyodyo dearest, I throw my arms around your neck and kiss
you a thousand times. I want you, I often do, to lift me in your
arms. But you always make excuses that I'm too heavy.

I don't want to write about business today—tomorrow, after seeing Kautsky. I'll go without the article because I'm waiting for your letter.

I hug you and kiss you on the mouth and on my belovedest nose and absolutely want you to carry me in your arms.

Yours Róża.

1. March 5 was L.'s twenty-ninth birthday.
2. J. never obtained the doctorate.
3. L.'s series of articles "Militia and Militarism," published in *Leipziger Volkszeitung* in February 1899, disputed M. Schippel's "crusade . . . in favor of the present military system. . . ." L. wrote, ". . . for capital, militarism is one of the most important forms of investment; from the point of view of capital, militarism is indeed a *relief* . . ." [*but not "from the point of view of workers"*].
4. For two different memories of L.'s Swiss vacations with J., see letters 17 and 66.

Letter 24

[Berlin]
[April 19, 1899]

Dyodyo! Finally I've got a free minute—I sent out the proofs and am exhausted—too tired to sleep. I have to write you now. For a long time I've wanted, actually needed, to tell you something, but there hasn't been a second!!

Do you know what I've been feeling very strongly? Something is moving inside me and wants to come out. It's something intellectual, something I must write. Don't worry, it's not poetry again or fiction. No, my treasure, it's in my brain that I feel something. I feel I haven't used a tenth or a hundredth part of my powers. I'm not happy with what I've been writing and absolutely and clearly know I can do much better work. In other words, as Heinrich says, I need to "say something important."

It's the *form* of my writing that no longer satisfies me. In my "soul" a totally new, original form is ripening that ignores all rules and conventions. It breaks them by the power of ideas and strong conviction. I want to affect people like a clap of thunder, to inflame their minds not by speechifying but with the breadth of my vision, the strength of my conviction, and the power of my expression.

How? What? Where? I still don't know.

Laugh to your heart's content, I don't care. I'm convinced that something is stirring inside me, something is being born. You're probably saying, "A great mountain goes into labor and a silly mouse is born." Never mind. We'll see.

I've been thinking again tonight about *your* situation, how and what to do? I'd give anything in the world, half of my life, to have it all settled. Oh, Dyodyo!

Write to me *every day*. I made a decision: to write to you daily, time permitting, even if it's only a line or two. It's dreadful that neither of us has had word of the other for *several* days.

My darling Dyodyuchny, I imagined you today awakened by a special delivery letter, crawling out of bed, cautiously sticking out your sleepy, blond disheveled head through the crack in the door, a silly look on your sweet face, and I was sorry I wasn't standing at the door so I could plant a kiss on that silly nose—so hard it hurts.

Rózia.

Leipzig got 600 copies of "Social Reform or Revolution" already. Three thousand will sell quickly, and I'll request royalties for the second edition.

I wrote back to Warski a long time ago and to the "Warsaw Library" as well.

Letter 25*

[Berlin]
Saturday
[May 27, 1899]

My golden Dyodyushka!

I just came back from Leipzig this morning and hasten to answer your dear letters and postcards, so you'll have this letter tomorrow morning. You're surprised, aren't you, that I stayed that long in Leipzig, but the Schönlanks, *she in particular,* received me so warmly, I just couldn't get away. On the first day she herself went to the railroad station and argued till my return ticket was extended from three to nine days and demanded that I stay with them the entire time. She hardly let me go today and only after a big fight.

We went to the theater three times: Wagner's *Rienzi,* Wagner Jr.'s *Bärenhäuter,* and *Der Widerspänstigen Zähmung* [*The Taming of the Shrew*] by Götz. It was quite a refreshing experience.

I met Haenisch[1] and his sister-in-law ([Mrs.] Sch[önlank's] good friend) who had worked for *Der Sozialdemokrat* at the time of the antisocialist laws. I also met Forker, the leading American socialist who stopped in Leipzig on his way to the Brussels' peace demonstration. I found out a great deal about the American movement from him. He read my pamphlet and will spread the word in his country.

The visit refreshed me, and I don't regret the time—anyhow, before going to Leipzig, I had been in no state to write anything decent. I keep thinking of the trip to Switzerland; I'm still worn out mentally, and I don't know if I can write anything decent before leaving for Switzerland. I'm afraid of writing trash again. Mill found me looking much thinner, and it worries me how you'll see me.[2] But if you're good to me and won't fight with me, I hope I will put on some weight in Zurich.

My whole trip [to Zurich] seems ill-starred. "Daddy's planning to leave in mid-June," they write me from home, but how this is supposed to work out God only knows. Today I'm writing them a firm letter: if daddy can't come in the beginning of June, we'll have to postpone his visit till the end of July. (In August at the latest, I must be back at work.) There's another reason why I want to go to Zurich as soon as possible. I don't know if I wrote you before going to L[eipzig] that I had seen Stadthagen and discussed my divorce with him (without of course telling him *who* it was, that is, Gustav [Lübeck]). He gave me some good advice, drafted the complaint, and most important urged me to file it at once, because as of January 1, 1900, a new German law will revoke the clause we want to plead: divorce on grounds of mutual incompatibility! The lawsuit itself may go on for a long time—that's why the complaint should be lodged immediately. Since nothing can be started without me, I must talk to Forrer at once.[3] Letters won't do.

As for my finances, I certainly find it much more unpleasant than you to keep asking you for help. I assure you I haven't spent a single penny on my own pleasures or out of negligence or sloppiness. I've lost a lot of money because of the fight I had with that shrew of a landlady. As usual, on the first I paid her a month in advance for room and board, and now my money is gone. I won't go to her myself, it isn't worth the headache it'll give me. I sent an acquaintance to her, and the landlady, fully aware I wouldn't bother with a lawsuit, told her I could take her to court. To make matters worse, I had rented the adjoining room for 15 M, planning to have the Kautskys and perhaps Mehring, etc. visit me in April. That money is lost, and in addition there was the cost of moving and of the three days I had spent in a hotel before finding another room. With the 100 M for April from Leipzig, I covered my current expenses. On the first I was left with about 70 M, and then two weeks ago my bookseller, Behr, started hounding me. He noticed I don't buy from him anymore and insisted I should pay at once the 40 M I owe him. I never wrote you that I had bought the third volume of Marx when I was working on Bernst[ein], and later a book on French cartels, and Hobson in English (*The Evolution of the Modern Capitalism*). Now everything has hit at once. Were it not for the moving, my accounts would have been in the best order. I assure you that in the future, after my return from Zurich, I will *never* ask for your help again. If, as you say, you are indeed more concerned with "order" than with money, let me add that first, even if I had the terrible vice of being "disorderly," this would be no disaster. Other women who earn no money, who have no particular intellectual or moral virtues are "disorderly," yet their husbands are very pleased with them and don't pick on them. Second, what you say is *not true* because my affairs are in such perfect order that others could learn from me. Your imprudent brother told me, in spite of my protests, about your finances.[4] Don't bother to write me about them; they're none of my concern. I know you'll always have enough for yourself; I, too, will always earn my keep and, if I have a child, I'll be able to support it by myself. You can spare yourself the cautious "hints" concerning your future income. [. . .]

I embrace you tenderly, you incorrigible creature! Remember me to your brother!

Yours R.

N.B. I got your registered letter now, after I came back.

* This letter, like that of August 2, 1899, is among the twenty-five letters recently discovered and published by Professor F. Tych in 1976. Archiwum Ruchu Robotniczego (*Warsaw: Książka i Wiedza, 1976*), vol. III, pp. 153–192.

1. Konrad Haenisch, SPD activist and journalist.
2. Josif Mill (John Mill) knew J. from the Wilno Jewish socialist movement. Founder of the *Bund* Committee Abroad he lived in exile in Switzerland and went to the USA in 1915.

3. R. Forrer, lawyer and sociologist, professor at the University of
Zurich. He and Stadthagen represented L. in her divorce case.
4. J. had a regular income from the family business in Wilno.

Postcard 26

Berlin
June 3, 1899

You horrid monkey!

Again you're furious! And why? Because I must wait a few
days for a letter from my father. You seem to forget that my
father hasn't seen me for 10 (ten) years. And from what I hear
about his health, it's clear that this is going to be our last
meeting. While you and I, thank god, will enjoy (and fight)
each other for another thirty years. You could show a little
more consideration for once. Too bad my poor father is not a
banker and can't take a vacation whenever he pleases, totally
dependent as he is on his penny's worth of miserable business.
As I wrote you, I'm leaving on *Wednesday,* and will meet my
father in *July.* He is very ill and I'll have to put him up in a
sanatorium. I'm on my way to K[autsky].

Kisses, though you aren't worth it.

Letter 27

[Gräfenberg]
August 2, 1899

Dyodyu, my golden one, I got your letters, No. 9 last night
and No. 10 today. Thanks for writing a few warm words at
last. I needed them badly, as I said in yesterday's postcard. I'm
sorry about my bitter tone, but, my dear love, it hurt that you
wrote only of business. Not a single loving word, and I was
feeling rotten. I still do. You don't know why. Well, let me tell
you.

My father isn't really sick—he's utterly exhausted physically and mentally. There's hardly a drop of blood left in him. He throws up, suffers from nausea, "faintness," burning in the throat, belching, cramps in the legs, coughing, all caused by his psychological state. He looks so dreadful that people stare at him. Back home those idiot doctors, including Józio, treated him with electricity and bromine and, instead of making him eat well, tortured him with a diet so that he was afraid to touch anything. This has been going on since mother's death—for almost two years.[1] Sick as he is, he *must* go about his business, day in day out, from morning till midnight, and you can imagine how he looked when he came.

I changed the whole treatment at once. I feed him everything he likes, mostly eggs (nine a day), milk, etc. He's already improving, but out of an old habit, he wakes up at night every two hours and coughs so neither of us can sleep. He gets up at 5 or 5:30 in the morning, so I too must get up, rub him with cold water (doctor's orders), make tea. After tea and a short rest, I boil the eggs, make coffee, wash the breakfast dishes, clean the room, get dressed, and go for a walk with him; a virtual ordeal because father creeps at a snail's pace (no exaggeration)—it sickens me. We have barely started walking when daddy is hungry again, and either I go back home and start cooking, or I take him out for a snack. Then we shuffle to lunch, and afterward it takes daddy a whole hour to get up to go home. After lunch I'd like to take a nap to get some rest, but daddy scarcely sleeps for fifteen minutes, and, as he wants his tea at once, I must get up. Half an hour later I'm making eggs and coffee again, then we drag ourselves for a walk, and it is the same all over again. I must cook at 5, at 7, and at 10 before he goes to bed. Then comes the night with coughing, jumping out of bed in the middle of the night, and *da capo al fine*.

Now all this is going on under the following conditions: *one* small room in an attic (!!) because we couldn't afford anything better; half of daddy's money and three-fourths of mine was spent on moving back and forth (Saltzbrunn, Carlsruh, Wroclaw [to find accommodations]). My "part" is separated by a screen. There's no place to move around. All I have is my gas burner and two small pans I use for cooking something else every minute, coffee, tea, eggs, milk, dumplings with milk—no sooner do I finish washing the dishes, than I start cooking all over again, unless I'm running around doing errands. Not a single hour for myself to read or at least write a letter. You can understand why my nerves are a bit strained. I myself don't even get a chance to eat with the gas burner constantly in use for daddy, and, sure enough, once I'm done with his food, it's time for a walk. Now imagine all these trips we made to find a suitable place for him, dragging heaps of bundles, his and mine, changing trains every hour, packing and unpacking, feeding daddy from a basket (I lugged it with me on the train), looking for rooms.

This is the first hour I snatched for myself because daddy met an acquaintance and went for a walk with him.

That's all I can tell you about myself. You asked where to send money and how much. Send as much as you can spare without putting yourself out; if worst comes to worst, I can ask for some from Leipzig. *My* address and my own name and an ordinary money order.

It's a pity you've been putting off sending me your ideas about France, because I'm going to try to start writing today. To keep silent in this matter is suicidal.[2]

You wanted to know why I had written to your brother—it was daddy's whim. Once he wrote to your brother from Warsaw to ask whether Segal's chemical factory and "The Wilno Chemical Factory" were one and the same. Ingeniously he addressed it to "Mr. Grozowski in Wilno."[3] Told it was a wrong address, he insisted I write again. Since he doesn't like to give up his whims, I wrote.

I have to stop for today—I must try to write this article.

I'll also write to Hamburg that they shouldn't count on me. I wrote to Sch[önlank].

I kiss you warmly, write often and more about yourself. Have you started your work??

Yours R.

Darlingest, if you can send us about 50 M, we could stay one week longer (till approximately the seventeenth).

1. After leaving Poland in 1889, L. never saw her mother again (Lina Luxemburg died in 1897). As she foresaw, this was her last meeting with her father. Elias Luxemburg died in 1900.
2. L. refers to the crisis in the French socialist movement over the Dreyfus affair and over socialist participation in bourgeois government.
3. Grozowski was one of J.'s pseudonyms; the best-known was Tyszka. After nine years of their relationship, L.'s father did not know J.'s real name.

Letter 28

[Berlin]
[September 24, 1899]

Dyodyu, my dear! Yesterday I sent my answer to P[arvus] to *L[eipziger] V[olkszeitung]*; you'll get it tomorrow. I'm pleased with it. It struck me today that I left a silly stylistic error, but I doubt anyone will notice. I'm going to ask *S[ächsische] A[rbeiterzeitung]* to reprint the whole article, and I'm sure they will.

As you see, *Vorwärts'* answer proves you wrong; they neither criticized my facts nor is there a hint of "mocking." Their tone is apologetic and crestfallen. Altogether the answer is so inept I wouldn't have expected it from Eisner.[1] As K[autsky] says, they're obviously scared of me. He was extremely pleased with my answer and considers it exceptionally sharp. So that's the end of that between *Vorwärts* and me. But I will

help Sch[önlank] write his riposte—he isn't very good at it.
I'll keep it between the two of us so he isn't publicly em-
barrassed.

I'm tired because of all that work (almost a month of it!) and
can see I'm not as much in control of my writing as I should
be. I decided to slow down and just write three things before
[the] Hanover [party congress]: (1) for *Pe[tite] Rép[ublique]*;
(2) for *Mouv[ement] Soc[ialiste]*; and (3) on elections to the local diet, probably for *Vorw[ärts]*.

I just got your long letter. Don't worry about me, I'm calm
and don't have much more work before Hanover.

Far away as you are, you can't have a real sense of my position in the party—it is *very* good. I sense it in K[autsky]'s attitude, in *Vorwärts'* response, in the entire party press. Now I
am completely sure of my position. If I still have many oppo-
nents among the "middle-of-the-roaders" (like *H[amburger]
Echo*), it's only because they don't quite understand me and
are afraid of me. However, just one more year of *constructive*
work, and my position will be excellent. In the meantime I
can't come out with a less radical speech since I represent the
most extreme wing. After Hanover I'll change my tone slightly.

Apropos, K[autsky] thinks that I am inciting Bebel in my articles for the party congress. "You've done it very cleverly!" he
laughed. He sees me as a future leader and wants to lean on
me. Let him! He's quite a monkey, but why should I care? *Pro
patria!* . . .

The bourgeois press is constantly chewing me out. But back
to my position. The enclosed *Nord[deutsche] Volksst[imme]*
will prove to you the impact my articles have on the party
congress. For the first time, they reprinted my articles. It's happening again—remember my articles about Bernstein? One
provincial paper after another picked them up—they're gradually accepting my views. In one year I hope to set the tone for

the whole party press (particularly after I soften my own tone). It doesn't take much. P[arvus] almost made it because the party doesn't have people with brains and character, and, if somebody appears who has both, the doors open wide. But Parvus managed to break his own neck and has made things difficult for *me*, too, into the bargain. It doesn't matter, they'll soon see I'm not P[arvus] and eventually will trust me.

As for Hanover, I feel calm and confident. I know what to do, and I count on success. I want you to know it, because you, my poor Dyodyo, are obviously very scared for me if, broke as you now are, you still want to come to H[anover]. But really there's nothing you can do to help me, and you'll just make yourself a nervous wreck as in Stuttg[art]. It's not Stuttg[art], and I'm not a novice anymore.[2] I won't disgrace myself.

But if you do *have* spare money and just want to stay with me during the congressional shindig, write *at once,* and I'll look for rooms, and not like the rooms in Stuttgart!

By the way, remember there'll be plenty of Russians in Hanover.

A pity neither of us knows the city, but we'll manage. Write *at once* what you decide!

Kisses.
Yours R.

1. Kurt Eisner, social democratic journalist, on the editorial board of *Vorwärts.* As L.'s radical ideas crystallized (". . . the only defenders of the extreme left are Kautsky and I. . . ," she wrote to J. on March 2, 1899), the opposition against her within the SPD grew, and she became increasingly isolated.
2. The SPD Stuttgart party congress in 1898 was L.'s "baptism by fire." J. went to Stuttgart then, but, unlike L., did not participate in the congress.

Letter 29

[Berlin]
Sunday
[December 17, 1899]

Dyodyu, my dear! I wanted to write you yesterday but was in the midst of the French articles, thinking them over and re-working them, and couldn't interrupt or I'd lose the thread.

My answer to Struve will appear in *N[eue] Z[eit]* in January,[1] as I arranged with K[autsky]. Why don't you take that issue of the *Archive* and read it carefully. You'll certainly come up with something I can use. For many and good reasons, this must be an elegant article. It is worth the effort!

I asked Schönlank about Hamburg; he used to live there. This plan isn't going to work out for one simple reason: the Hamburg climate is very harsh and foggy, similar to England's, so with your chronic cold it doesn't make sense to ask for more trouble. Besides, in the summer there's nothing there but the sea, which is bad for both of us; brisk air and cold baths are not for nervous people. Otherwise, conditions are good there, but, as far as I'm concerned, the reasons above take care of the matter. What a drastic change of climate, especially for you coming straight from Switzerland!

Instead, I have a different idea—Heidelberg! A delightful town, wonderful nature, hilly countryside, on the Neckar, we could either make regular day trips in the summer or else rent a flat nearby. The university library is famous, but most important is the town: first, it's in *Hessen* where the police are very decent; second, ever since the celebrated doctor Rüdt's time, there has been no vestige of any party movement! We'd be free from comrades and gossip. Besides, it's a big town, lo-cated in the center of Germany (eight hours from Berlin) and with all kinds of cultural entertainments. Think it over and write back. Remember, it's very important for us to make the best of the summers and to *recover physically.* [. . .]

Your advice to "force" my brothers to support my father is of course superb; too bad it's pointless. On the whole, you have too much faith in the magic power of the word "force" in both politics and personal life. I, for one, have more faith in the power of the word "do." [. . .]

The Kautskys invited me for Christmas Eve, but I didn't accept and will stay home. My landlords, with whom I'm very friendly, invited me for a family dinner. This, I suppose, is the last Christmas Eve we won't celebrate together.[2] Good Lord, when I think about our first years together, what kind of holidays did we have even then! We never knew how to celebrate holidays. You know, there are no holidays without children, no real family life. Don't you think so?

We'll be in an empty house forever. . . . More and more often I *seriously* think of adopting a child. This would be possible only if we've a regular income and sufficient means. Will I be too old then to raise a child?

I constantly feel the need for a child—sometimes it gets unbearable. *You* probably could never understand this.

I'm pleased that you stayed at the Kohler-woman's [landlady] after all. You're used to your four walls, and it would be unpleasant to move again, to find a new place. Stay where you are till you come to live with me.

Fond kisses. Yours R.

1. Piotr B. Struve, Russian economist and philosopher, leader of Russian liberals, the most prominent exponent of "legal Marxism" in Russia.
2. Unlike other socialists (Kautsky, Bebel), L. attached importance to traditional holidays like Christmas and Easter throughout her life. See *August Bebel's Briefwechsel mit Karl Kautsky,* Karl Kautsky, Jr. ed. (Assen: Van Gorcum & Comp. N.V., 1971).

Letter 30

[Berlin]
[ca. January 13, 1900]

Dyodyu, my dear! You are really quite funny! First you write me an obnoxious letter, and then you respond to my cursory answer with "the tone of your postcard hardly puts me in a mood to write at greater length. . . ."

You don't seem to see that all your letters are systematically and colossally distasteful; they boil down to one long, drawn-out stuffy *mentorship* like "the letters of a schoolmaster to his favorite pupil." Granted, you make critical comments; granted, they are generally useful, even in some cases indispensable, but, for heaven's sake, by now the whole thing has become a *disease,* an addiction! I can't put a single idea or fact on paper without provoking a boring, distasteful harangue. No matter what I'm writing about, my articles, my visits, my newspaper subscriptions, dresses, family relations, anything I care about and share with you—none of it escapes your advice and directions. I swear to god this is getting to be boring! Even more so because it is one-sided. You never give me your work to criticize, not that I care to instruct you. I don't have the poor taste to do so and, even if I did, you wouldn't listen anyhow. For instance, what sense does yesterday's tirade of yours make: "concerning your tasks in the German movement and your political writing on the one hand, and on the other your household duties, *in order not to go to the dogs both spiritually and politically. . .*"?

I'd be more interested in your telling me what you assigned yourself "concerning tasks?" What are you reading in order not to go to the dogs? Judging by the spirit and content of your letters, I'm afraid it seems more likely that *you* will "go to the dogs" in Zurich than I will in Berlin. It's distasteful—saving me every few weeks from "going to the dogs!"

All this comes from your old addiction—to moralize—
which, from the beginning in Zurich, made me miserable and
has completely spoiled our lives. You seem to feel called upon
to preach at me and to play the role of my mentor always, no
matter what. Your current advice and criticism of my "activities" go far beyond a close friend's comments—it's just systematic moralizing. God knows, all that's left for me to do is
to shrug my shoulders and cut my letters to a minimum lest
they provoke further disgusting sermons.

Besides, how can I trust your moralizing when, most often,
it depends on your mood. Let me give you a little example:
last week I complained to you that, unintentionally or even
against my better judgment, I got involved in a personal
friendship with the Kautskys. You said that this friendship
made you *very happy*. Fine. Then, in response to my letter
about my visit with the Kautskys, which certainly wasn't sent
to elicit your "critical analysis," you went into a long and profound discourse about the futility and harmfulness of a friendship with the Kautskys. How do you reconcile these two
views? It's simple—the first time you were in a good mood, the
second, in a rotten one. Then, right away, you start painting everything black and begin saving me from "going to the dogs."

One more thing. I'm only impressed by principles and advice that the adviser follows himself. Along with your advice,
do, please, let me know how things are with *you* (for instance,
how your [doctoral] thesis is progressing, how systematic your
intellectual work is, what "homeland" newspapers you subscribe to and read, etc., etc.).

I laid you out in lavender, didn't I! See! Every dog has his
day, many a pickle makes a mickle, don't stick your head in a
noose, the pot calls the kettle black—there are many more
pure Polish proverbs I could go on quoting were I not afraid
you couldn't understand the finesse of the Polish language. So
let me just add one more saying composed by Mr. Jowialski [a
character in a classic Polish play]: the older the cat, the

tougher his tail. . . . You're smart enough to draw your own
conclusions for, as we say in Poland, a word to the wise is
sufficient.

[. . .] Affectionate hugs!

Yours Rózia.

Letter 31

[Berlin]
[ca. January 22, 1900]

My dear Dyodyu! I wanted to write you a long letter, but
again I got news from father that left me drained—I can deal
with urgent matters only!

Let me explain about the job at K[autsky's]. It involves shar-
ing the editorship with him: editing a part of the manuscripts,
maintaining contact with the contributors, writing "Notes" if
no one else does, and occasionally writing book reviews.
Writing articles is not included. Working hours: morning till
noon, three or four times a week.

The job is not that of a private secretary to K[autsky], but of
the editor of N[eue] Z[eit], hired not by K[autsky] but by J. H. W.
D[ietz][1] (G.m.b.H.), that is, by Dietz, Singer, and Bebel.

I mentioned it to K[autsky] noncommittally; he was very
pleased and immediately talked to Dietz and Bebel. Bebel said
he could imagine no one better than me for N[eue] Z[eit]. Dietz
likewise. There's one problem—they must find another job for
Cunow and are still looking for it.[2] Cunow's salary was 200 M
monthly, but Dietz wanted to cut it. I told K[autsky] I wouldn't
take a lower salary than Cunow.

Now, in view of father's condition, I want this job badly, but
where the hell can anyone find a position for Cunow?

As for our plans, of course we must live together in Berlin. I
didn't start thinking about this after you reminded me; I have
been thinking about it for a long, long time.

You write that the part-time job with Kautsky is something unusual. You're wrong. I had almost gotten a job at Hayman's library, two hours a day, 180 M monthly, but it turned out they needed a professional librarian. In a big city with some effort and some connections, part-time jobs are available, and it's clear that we cannot manage without an additional income.

You think that my plans to earn money threaten my scholarly and political future. You're wrong. I'd need more time to explain. Anyhow, it isn't all that bad. I, for one, follow the principle that people's *primary* concern is to support themselves and their children or their parents, *and only then* should they think of becoming great scholars. Besides—*sind's Rosen, nun sie werden blühen* [if they're roses, they'll bloom]. No genuine talent ever flourished because it devoted *all* it's time to self-development.

As to *what* arrangements should be made here, all I know is that furnished rooms scare me out of my wits. There is time, I suppose, to talk about details; however, I'd like to know *when* you're coming.

Apropos the job at K[autsky's], it includes one month of summer vacations, or two, or three, as I please, as long as I don't leave at the *same time* as K[autsky]—we'll work it out.

My connections have already proved a bit helpful to the "Polish cause."[3] A few weeks ago Kautsky received an article about Poland from Płochocki and asked me what I think of Płochocki. He wanted to know how I'd react if he published it. Naturally I politely let him know, and the article vanished. I hope it won't be published. Send Struve back, *soon.*

Affectionate kisses.

Róża.

1. J. H. W. Dietz, active in the SPD, owner of a publishing house in Stuttgart which printed *Neue Zeit.*
2. Heinrich Cunow, sociologist, journalist, member of the SPD. Eventually he became a revisionist.

3. L. meant it ironically. L. Płochocki, cofounder of the PPS and its leading publicist, advocated Poland's independence, and was subsequently in opposition to the SDKPiL and L. (See appendix.)

Letter 32

[Berlin]
March 15, [19]00

My dear! I fell ill on my way to Stuttgart and stayed over Monday at [Clara] Zetkin's to get some rest, left Tuesday morning and arrived here at 11 P.M. Found Marchlewski's letter and an old postcard at home.

I've carefully considered our present situation and have come to the following conclusion: The only hope for a mutual agreement and a more-or-less-normal relationship is to live together in Germany. I don't know and can't think why you keep putting it off, but I do know this postponement is abnormal and humiliating to me.

I'm not willing to be party to a situation I neither understand nor recognize, and, since I see no possibility of reaching an understanding with you until we settle here, further letters from me are absolutely pointless. I trust you'll think it over and agree with me and won't expect any letters from me until your arrival. I'll write only if business requires it.

Yours R.

Letter 33

[Berlin]
March 29, [19]00

My dear! I came from Poznań so tired that I couldn't hold a pen in my hand until today.

I'll answer your letter briefly. At first, having read your letter, I felt like telling you everything, reporting on my trip and explaining my urgent departure, etc., from *my* point of view, just as I used to do in the old days. But it occurred to me that for eight years I've been doing this to no avail, so I gave up. I'm going to write only about what deals with further plans, with facts.

Your letter made it clear that only your lack of wanting to prevents you from moving to Berlin; there are no other unfathomable reasons. If a person feels no need for a permanent union, it is, I think, simply a lack of inner courage to carry on a marital relationship at a distance or on fleeting visits. Berlin, as such, means nothing. If you see no reason, no purpose to moving here with me, there is no way we can go on living as we lived, even temporarily, in Zurich. Even to correspond in the manner we used to is no longer possible.

Your suggestion that I come to Zurich solely to stir your desire to move to Berlin is strange, to say the least—I wonder how it's possible you didn't realize it. Perhaps you won't understand my response either. I cannot explain it to you. I can only assure you I will never set foot in Zurich, nor will I go to any other place to see you. . . .

It's entirely up to you how soon, if ever, you will feel sufficiently driven to settle here, near me. I can't and I don't want to interfere in any way, not even with letters.

As for my health, I'll let you know if there's an emergency. The same goes for my financial needs—in an emergency I'll get in touch with you. (N.B. Since I came back from Zurich about the fifteenth and made the trip to Poznań, I've barely earned half of my living expenses. If you can spare it, I could use 50 M by the 1st.)

One more thing. My decision to stop writing is not the act of vengeance you think it is. It's not a boycott either. It's simply the need finally to get out of that charmed circle of riddles. I've been spinning around in it for too long.

Yours Róża.

Letter 34

[Berlin]
April 24, 1900

Dyodyu, my dear! Your letter came just in time, just as I was desperately trying to figure out when this turmoil between us would end.

To explain my recent attitude and behavior, let me tell you briefly: what has been going on between us of late—especially my visit to Zurich—has led me to believe that you . . . stopped loving me, that you might even be involved with someone else, that I was no longer the one who could make you happy, if it is possible to make you happy at all.

This thought struck me that night when I was lying on the sofa at [Clara] Zetkin's. I couldn't sleep—thoughts kept crowding in on me. Then suddenly everything was crystal clear— your reluctance to come to Berlin, your recent behavior—in the light of *this* fact it became understandable, and, so help me god, I breathed freely. I felt like someone who, after endless riddles, tangles, jumbles, and confusion, at last finds the clear though most painful answer to *all* questions. At once I decided to make the parting easier for you. I'd stop writing to you so I wouldn't influence your mood or create new ties. I kept telling myself this was the solution: If he loves me and wants us to live together, he'll come, if not—he can take advantage of the break in our correspondence, slowly detach himself and let the relationship "dissolve."

So I started to live in complete solitude, knowing that I am, and always will be, alone. It made me feel slightly cold but proud, too. How many times when I watched other people together, how many times when I felt the beauty of being alive in the spring—I felt deeply that you'd never find anyone with whom you could live *the life* that you can live with me . . . . And I would begin to weave new plans and hopes. Yet each time a single, simple thought would sneak in: *He* is already living a different life, and you have nothing to give *him*. This thought was enough to sweep the mirages away and send me back to my work with clenched teeth.

Judging by your letter it seems that—that I was wrong (I too am incapable of spelling out certain words) and that there's a foundation and a hope for our relationship. But are you sure of yourself? Are you fully aware of what's going on within you? Isn't it inertia? Dyodyu! . . .

But if everything really is all right, don't tell me what happened or why, just tell me when and how we're going to arrange our life. This is urgent for many reasons.

Now briefly about other things. Dyodyu, my dear, if I "pushed" you out of my affairs, it was *only* because I felt guilty about burdening you with the Polish work. I told myself if I didn't stop doing that, I'd ruin you forever—and only out of plain egoism. Remember how often you've told me that in order to keep our relationship normal, you must know I can get along without you?! Well, I did everything I could to manage by myself, to free you from me. And you took it for "pushing you out"?! . . . If only you knew how hard it is for me to have no one to give me advice, no one to lean on or share my doubts with. But I suppressed this feeling, thinking I shouldn't drag you into my affairs—it would be deadly for you. If you only wanted to, how delightfully we could work and live together! There's plenty of work, and I can't handle even one-tenth all by myself.

Now, in addition to the German work, I have the Polish work, too. It's impossible to describe the meeting.[1] I must tell you about it. For two whole days a fight raged against me. But I dominated the whole meeting, and finally they put themselves into my hands. Since at the editor's request I covered the second day for *Vorwärts*, I could hardly advertise myself, and besides I didn't want to provoke the losers. In effect, complete victory on all fronts; I even won over the most implacable enemies. This caused a virtual panic in the intelligentsia wing of the PPS. They're already trying to distort events, as you can see from the article in *The Workers' Journal,* which I enclosed (send it back *at once*). My answer will appear in the next issue.

My review of Schüller's book will appear in *Neue Zeit.* I was honored twice: (1) K[autsky] gave me the French translation of his work against Bernstein and inscribed it to *Meiner lieben Freundin* R . . . L . . .—K . . . K . . . ; (2) he asked if I'd agree to edit Marx's manuscripts in case Marx's legacy contains more manuscripts than just the fourth volume of *Das Kapital.* Of course I agreed. In a few days he's going to Paris to take over the legacy from Lafargue.

I haven't written much for *L[eipziger] V[olkszeitung]* because first there was the Poznań trip, then my illness (I was laid up for a week), then this meeting. I just sent off the third article, am finishing the fourth, and with the fee from *Neue Zeit* will balance my budget.

The other day in Poznań was a success: I wrecked a Catholic meeting and spoke at three meetings—shoemakers, tailors, and a party meeting. [. . .]

I go to K[autsky] rarely and stay briefly—more often he comes to my place—they bore me to tears. In general, mankind makes me want to throw up, and you, you wicked, mean creature, make my heart ache.

When will you stop dawdling in Switzerland?!

Kiss you on the mouth!

Yours R.

The news from my family is painful, but let's not talk about it.

1. The Fifth Congress of the Polish Socialist Party (PPS) in German-annexed Poland, held in Berlin.

Letter 35

[Berlin]
Monday
[April 30, 1900]

Dyodyu, my dear! [. . .] Yes, you are quite right. We've
been living separate spiritual lives for a long time. But it didn't
start in Berlin. Even in Zurich we were spiritual strangers, and
the frightful loneliness of these last two years is engraved on
my mind. But *I* was not the one who withdrew, who shut myself off. Exactly the opposite. You ask if I've ever asked myself
how *you* live, what's happening inside *you*? All I can do is
smile bitterly. Yes, I did ask. I asked myself thousands of times,
and I asked *you* again and again, loudly, insistently only to get
the same answers, always the same—that I don't understand
you, that you can't count on me, that I am incapable of giving.
Finally I stopped asking and never showed that I was con-
scious of or interested in anything. Now you ask how I could
ever think you were attracted to another woman, since no
woman but me is capable of responding to you, of understanding you. Exactly what I had told myself in the past.

You have forgotten, haven't you, that you kept repeating
over and over again that I, too, don't understand you, that you
feel utterly lonely with me as well. Then what's the difference?
This realization brought home to me that I don't exist for you
anymore. So my reaction to the same doubts was different in
1893? Of course it was. I've changed since then. I was a mere
child, now I am an adult, a mature person in perfect control of
myself, capable of gritting my teeth in pain, of showing nothing, absolutely nothing. But you, no matter what, refuse to believe that I have changed, that I am not the same person I was
eight years ago.

One more thing. You persistently ask how I can write off
our relationship so casually. The "casually" I don't want to

discuss. How did I manage to do it? Here's the secret: My last
visit to Zurich left me with no shade of doubt that you've
grown utterly blind to me, to my inner being, that all I am for
you is just another woman, perhaps different from others in
that I write articles. Here in Berlin I constantly see *the kind of
women* men live with, how those men worship them and yield
to their domination, and all the time, in the back of my mind,
I am aware of the way you treat me. After a long time I finally
understood that you had lost all sensitivity to me, to my inner
being. Indeed, you have even lost all memory of it. This, more
than anything else, made me acutely and painfully aware that
deep inside you had grown cold.

You ask if I *want* to renew our common spiritual life? The
answer is clear, but, remember, its realization depends on *you*.
It is impossible to build a *common* spiritual life if we continue
to live as we do. An agreement between us is possible only if
you get rid of your mistrust and if you believe that I'm capable
of understanding you and that I do care about your inner life.

There are so many, many things I want to tell you, but god
knows I don't have the strength to write. Once you are here,
once we start living at last, we'll tell each other everything.
But perhaps then words won't be necessary.

I'll write to Forrer one of these days; the divorce drags on
and on. Considering future arrangements, why not go back to
the original plan: settle in the South for half a year. Here it's
impossible to live openly together, and short of that, our life
will turn into a caricature I fear more than loneliness. We
need peace in order to live, and we cannot find it hiding.
Think about it. How are things with Anna? I haven't written to
her, you know why.

Hundred kisses.

R.

Letter 36

[Berlin]
Wednesday
[May 2, 1900]

Dearest Dyodyu! I got your short letter yesterday; again business. My golden heart, again you got heated up because of some nonsense (the comment in *Vorwärts*) and suggest that I move heaven and earth and the executive committee and so on. Remember, we've repeatedly promised ourselves not to blow up over every trifle. The comment in *Vorwärts* is fiddle-sticks, not worth a damn. You're imagining that it's aimed *against* us. Second, remember we decided to change our tactics with the local Poles. We agreed not to attack them via the Germans and the German press but, on the contrary, *to win their confidence.* Now you're pressing me to set up a German demonstration against them. Is this consistent? One must stick to something and not jump from one tightrope to another! I've taken the first steps to gain the trust of the local people, so don't tell me to do an about-face.

I'd be most pleased if you used half of the energy, passion, and persistence you're spending on the PPS on our personal life, that is, on settling your affairs in Zurich, on your doctorate, on making arrangements for our future. Since our reconciliation, I've had four letters from you, three about the PPS, one about us, but nothing about practical matters.

I've been racking my brains to figure out where and how we could live openly as husband and wife. If we don't, the whole thing isn't worth a damn. For heaven's sake, try to understand I can't put my father off any longer. Relying on your promises, I told my father last summer that we would be living together by this spring. For the past month I have been at a loss about what to tell father and have been lying like a crook. It's high time to end this procrastination.

I see no reason for your staying on in Zurich. The affair with Gust[av] may drag on for god knows how long, and we can't wait forever. Should your presence in Zurich be really needed later on, a sacrifice of 60 M *will get you there.* Forget the money—we're losing more than 60 M by living apart, so it'll even out.

You must write to your brother that you're about to marry me so he can plan his trip in time.

As you said yourself, you'll need two to three weeks to take care of the odds and ends in Zurich. There's no doubt you should sell the printing press. (N.B. You don't have a matrix, do you? Don't forget to answer.)

Now concerning Gustav. It's impossible to wait for news from Forrer, therefore, my treasure, do the following: Go to the district court on Flössergasse, ask for Herr Doctor Billeter, introduce yourself as my brother or cousin and ask what's going on with my case and the federal court's decision. He said the decision would take three to four weeks at most and it has been three months now.

Do it and do it now. At least we'll know where we are.

I'm angry with you because you never stop scribbling about the PPS but haven't said a word about our reunion. I *do not understand,* or am afraid to.

> I embrace you affectionately,
> Yours R.

Letter 37

[Berlin]
[ca. May 9, 1900]

My dear! This morning I got another long letter from you about *The Workers' Journal,* etc. I wrote last night that I'll send an answer following your advice, so it's pointless to dwell on it.

I also wrote you about your doctorate yesterday. However, your last letter made me change my mind. To leave Zurich after ten years without a doctorate would be very unpleasant indeed. The only way out I can see is to stay in Zurich and work until you've finished. But I beg you to stop this never-ending irresolution, this back-and-forth business, and *make a decision*—decide how long you're going to stay in Zurich—and, having made up your mind, send me your *final* and *definite* word. I expect your final and *definite decision* in approximately four days.

Kisses.
R.

Your letter to Krichevsky could hurt your reputation enormously. It's brutal and incautious. If the content is a slap in the face, the manner should be subtle.

Letter 38

[Berlin]
Friday evening
[May 25, 1900]

Dyodyunka, my love!

[. . .] Kautsky keeps pressing me for articles for *N[eue] Z[eit]*, and I'm getting sick of it. N.B. The day before yesterday, they invited me for dinner again, and he took the opportunity to ask if I'd help him work on Marx's fourth volume [of *Das Kapital*]. It didn't take me long to find out what this "work" meant: He's transcribing the whole manuscript (terribly illegible) and intends to put it in order later on. Obviously my "help" would consist in transcribing or in taking his dictation. He's anxious for me to do it because, he said, after Engels' death, except for E. B[ernstein], he's the only person left who can read Marx's handwriting. He wants to initiate me into

Marx's hieroglyphs, so that were he to die while working on
the fourth volume, I'd continue the work (! . . .). He is much
too honest and simple a man to have consciously tried to trick
me into doing the copying, but *unconsciously* that naive story
about his possible death had no other purpose. Knowing full
well that neither our contemporaries nor posterity would ever
learn about my silent contribution to Marxism, I told him
straight out, I'm nobody's fool! Of course, I put it in an elegant
form, that is, poking fun at his fear and assuring him it would
be pointless to teach me Marx's handwriting, since my
chances of a sudden death are the same as his. I also advised
him to buy a Remington typewriter and to teach his wife to
type.

Apropos, you ask why I'm "at odds" with her. I'm not. On
the contrary, she loves me enormously, kisses me all the time,
addresses me as *du.* But I've been observing her, and I don't
like her character. She's very much like the Kalmansonov
woman [Pavel Akselrod's sister-in-law], only more sure of herself. That type of *woman* puts me off. I expect nobility in
women and she has none.[1] *Hinc illae lacrimae* [hence those
tears] and that's all.

I went to a good ladies' tailor whom my landlady knows
from her better days. In a week, for Whitsuntide, I'll have my
black skirt ready, and after the holidays, the yellow dress. I
also ordered a nice little hat with a feather, English style, modest but elegant. It'll be delivered on Saturday.

What I get from N[eue] Z[eit] this month will cover my living expenses, but it won't be enough to pay for the tailor and
for the hat. [. . .]

Have a nice Sunday!
Yours R.

1. Luise Kautsky became one of L.'s closest friends. In 1923 she
published Luxemburg's *Briefe an Karl und Luise Kautsky,* followed

by *Rosa Luxemburg, Ein Gedenkenbuch* in 1929. Fleeing Nazi-occu-
pied Austria, Luise Kautsky rescued other of L.'s letters, which
her son, Benedikt Kautsky, published in 1950 as *Briefe an Freunde,*
"to fulfill my mother's wish."

Postcard 39

[Berlin]
[May 31, 1900]

Dyodyushya, golden one!

I'll write tomorrow about the Polish affairs. Bebel's speech
dropped a new topic in my lap—trade unions and politics. It's
darn difficult. I'm trying to decide if I should start on it now.
The trouble is I'm now working on the article for the Paris
congress. I had a letter from Poznań inviting me to a meeting.
It's an opportunity to obtain a mandate both to Mainz and to
Paris. I can't wait to hear what you'll say about my article on
obstructionism.[1] I need about 15 M for the tailor to pay for the
black skirt (sewing, lining, and accessories), about 23 M for
the yellow dress (sewing, trimming, and accessories), and I
think not more than 8 M for the hat! I don't walk around like
a ragamuffin but look extremely neat (freshly laundered
blouses with the black skirt; the summer hat from last year
with a veil, still decent looking, will do for every day). Yesterday I sent your picture home. My landlady accidentally saw it
lying on the table and immediately announced she's ready to
divorce her husband for you. Dyodyu, write more.

A big kiss.
Yours R.

1. "Bilanz der Obstruktion" ["A balance sheet of obstruction"],
published in *Neue Zeit* on May 2, 1900.

Postcard 40

[Berlin]

[June 9, 1900]

Dear Dyodyu, your long letter really irritated me. It was full of your old conceit and that self-assurance that insists you know better than the whole world. As for Gustav [Lübeck], last year's version won't do; what is needed is *some common* incident that surely happened anyhow during the last year.[1] You don't have to tell him about the court evidence nor does he have to mention it to that woman. Your fear that a hired, registered prostitute might refuse to "confess" in court is just ridiculous. Stadthagen is an old hand at this kind of lawsuit, and I must listen to him, not to you. Please, please don't try to be smarter and shrewder than everyone else. I've sent you a copy of the letter;[2] so get in touch with G[ustav], *get it done* and don't criticize. What you say about my losing influence with Sch[önlank] is rubbish. Everybody's determined to upset me.

I don't kiss you.

Yours R.

1. The altered divorce law (letter 25) required evidence of Luxemburg's husband's infidelity. L. inferred that in the course of a year Lübeck was with a prostitute. This is the "incident" that "surely happened anyhow." "Gustav mustn't *do* anything," she explained to Jogiches two days earlier, "he must only *refresh his memory.*"
2. The lawyer, Stadthagen, drafted a letter from Lübeck to Luxemburg that was to serve her as legal proof in the divorce case.

Letter 41

[Berlin]

[ca. July 3, 1900]

Dyodyo, my beloved! How badly I need you! How badly we need each other! By god, no other couple has a task like ours: to shape a *human being* out of each other. I feel it every moment, and this makes our separation even more painful.

The two of us constantly "live" an inner life. It means we keep changing and growing, and this creates an inner dissociation, an imbalance, a disharmony between some parts of our souls and others. Therefore, the inner self must be constantly reexamined, readjusted, harmonized. One must constantly work on oneself to avoid sinking into spiritual consuming and digesting. But in order not to lose the overall sense of existence that I believe is a life committed outward, constructive action, creative work, one needs the control of another human being. That human being must be close, understanding and yet separate from the "I" that seeks harmony.

I doubt this makes much sense to you—it seems more like a sequence of algebraic symbols. It is in fact the one-hundredth link in the chain of thoughts and emotions stirred by the following painful experience: the honorable editor of *L[eipziger] V[olkszeitung]* sent back my article (a neutral topic—the war in China) along with a polite note excusing me from further collaboration.

Knowing Sch[önlank] only too well, I was sure this was bound to happen once my personal relationship with him was over. The long interruption in my collaboration was probably the immediate reason, though I explained I had been ill. But even earlier I had no doubt there was no future for me in *Leipziger Volkszeitung.* Anyhow, they wouldn't publish anything of mine reflecting my own *ideas.* Example: for *L[eipziger] V[olkszeitung]* my article about obstructionism had to be diluted and toned down.

Still, the accomplished fact did hurt me. You'll appreciate it, of course, though you'll go too far in your pessimism. Besides the political problem, the financial one is constantly hanging over my head—how and where to make some money?! But let's not lose our heads and composure; more tragic things happen in personal and in political life.

> Hundreds of kisses.
> Yours R.

Letter 42

> [Berlin]
> Thursday
> [July 26, 1900]

Dyodyonushka, my golden!

You've no idea how happy your personal letter made me. It came the day before yesterday. I read it over and over again. Tomorrow after you've delivered your paper, your term will be over. Now I do nothing but wait for the date of your arrival! There's only one thing that worries me: your paper may be too long to give in a single session (even in two hours), and you'll stay on for another week!

No, it doesn't make me laugh, it makes me happy that you applied yourself with such passion to your paper, or rather to your doctorate.[1] Working on it, you've realized how well you can write (both in general and in German), something you never believed when I told you.[2] Also, the doctorate will encourage you to try your hand at other kinds of work. For a long time I've planned to divide the work here between the two of us, reading according to a schedule, complementing each other's writing.

I'm constantly in touch with my family and my letters are always about us. Listen to what I hit upon to avoid a "wedding ceremony" and all kinds of related troubles. I wrote that since you're a Swiss citizen, our marriage must take place on Swiss territory; therefore, I must go to Switzerland. Since there's little time left and for them to get there from Warsaw would be difficult, I'll go there alone, and then we'll have a wedding reception in Germany. They agreed at once, so we don't have to "get married." You know how I dislike making up such tales, but what else is there to do? This way, I suppose, we'll avoid most of the trouble. As soon as you come, we'll discuss the family reunion. You'll see how much you'll like them. My wardrobe is in excellent shape. I don't need anything for my "trousseau." I look very elegant, have a different dress every Sunday.

Dyodyu, my only one, I beg you, let me know the date of your arrival ahead of time. If you surprise me, I'll either embarrass myself in front of the maid and my landlords, or feign restraint and that will spoil our first minute together. But if you tell me in advance, we'll arrange everything to make the most of it. So do write when you're coming!! And don't forget to bring *your pillow*. You mean creature, of course now you'll start rushing around with a hundred and one affairs, there'll be Gustav, and transportation, and the packing of books, etc. It will take you another week again![3] I'm waiting for the news about your paper! Thousand kisses!

Yours R.

Dyodyu, before you leave, go and get a remnant of raw silk for about 15 Fr for a dress for me and a piece for a blouse (a present for my sister).

1. As mentioned before, J. never obtained a doctoral degree nor did he write a doctoral dissertation. What L. refers to was a term paper.
2. Many years later L. wrote to Konstantin Zetkin: "His brilliance and intelligence notwithstanding, Leo is simply unable to write. The mere thought of putting his ideas on paper paralyzes him." Róża Luksemburg, *Listy do Leona Jogichesa-Tyszki*, F. Tych, ed. (Warsaw: Książka i Wiedza, 1968), vol. I, p. XXXVIII.
3. L. wrote her last letter to J. in Zurich on August 4th.

Together
1900–1906

If in some of her letters Luxemburg seems like a German Hausfrau in a household complete with husband and a maid-servant, it only means that "the formidable Rosa," as she remarked in a different context, was "quite human." Yet housekeeping and entertaining were never anything but a distraction after hard, absorbing work; they should not be mistaken for more than that.

Jogiches, a commander without troops on alien ground, left Berlin at the end of 1901 to accompany his dying, tuber-cular brother to Algiers. When he returned in the spring of 1902, he moved into the apartment Rosa had found in the meantime in Friedenau, a residential section of Berlin, an apartment, she said, that "feels like a real home." It felt less so after she broke with Jogiches and he still claimed it as his (letter 75).

But life on the move was over; the wandering, the home-lessness, the furnished rooms. "I like to stay at home most of all and just stare at the nice rooms. . . ." And yet, "it is so empty and silly at home without children," she wrote to Algiers, "and I feel so lonely. It seems to me I'd come back to life if I had a child. Meanwhile, I'd like at least a dog or a cat." (January 3, 1902) At the time their closeness began to disintegrate, she acquired a puppy and informed Jogiches

that "Puck wouldn't let 'mama' leave him for a single moment." (July 31, 1905)

In the years preceding the 1905 Russian revolution, Luxemburg grew into a national figure in the SPD. As a radical
Marxist politician, however, she found herself increasingly
at odds with the more conservative wing in the SPD. Not
that it was a setback. Impervious to personal abuse—whether
for her "petticoat politics," or as a "cantankerous woman,"
or an "uprooted Jewess"—she fought her sometimes lonely
battle unperturbed. "You'd better get used to it *once and
forever,*" she comforted the enraged Jogiches, that ". . . nothing can make me respond *now or ever* . . . to such dirt . . . ;
it would be degrading and I refuse to respond, even if it's
only my whim. And please, my love, don't ever advise me
to write volumes in self-defense. One may do it in three
words or, best, not at all." (December 5, 1899)

She kept canvassing that part of Poland annexed by Germany, sending the news to Algiers that ". . . by now the
most popular name in Poland is mine . . ." (January 22, 1902);
attending the SPD congresses in Mainz, Munich, and Jena;
participating in congresses of the Socialist International in
Paris, Brussels, and Amsterdam; regularly contributing to
Leipziger Volkszeitung (for several months as joint editor) and
to *Neue Zeit,* her influence on editorial policy steadily increas-
ing; delivering dozens of speeches and lectures; and publishing articles and pamphlets (over 200 between 1900–1905). The
editorship of *Leipziger Volkszeitung,* though offered to her, did
not materialize evidently for fear that she would "go overboard in party polemics" (letter 50, n.6).

In 1904 in her article "Organizational Questions of Russian
Social Democrats," she began a polemic questioning Lenin's
policies. One of the first on the European scene to recognize
Lenin's political genius, she was a supporter and at the same
time a critic of the Bolsheviks. As she wrote, "The 'discipline'
Lenin has in mind is implanted in the proletariat not only by

the factory but equally so by the *barracks*, by the modern bureaucracy, in sum, by the entire mechanism of the centralized bourgeois state apparatus. . . . The ultracentralism advocated by Lenin is permeated in its very essence by the sterile spirit of a nightwatchman [*Nachtwächtergeist*] rather than by a positive and creative spirit. He concentrates mostly on *controlling* the party, not on *fertilizing* it, on *narrowing* it down, not *developing* it, on *regimenting* not on *unifying* it." [1] Their differing views on the means and goals of the revolution did not diminish the respect they had for each other. "Lenin came yesterday and called on me four times in two days," Luxemburg would write later to Konstantin Zetkin. "It's a pleasure to talk to him. He is sophisticated and knowledgeable, with that kind of ugly face I like so much to look at. . . ." (February 1912). She was not to complete her polemic till 1918 with an assessment of the first year of Lenin's reign, posthumously published in 1922 as *Die Russische Revolution.*

The year 1904 also gave her the first taste of prison, which made her promise herself "to live life to its full" once she was free (letter 57). She was sentenced for insulting Emperor Wilhelm II in one of her speeches. But it was less her fight against the emperor than the struggle against Jogiches's "spritual suicide" that had been wearing her down.

The 1905 revolution in Russia, which soon swept over Poland, subdued the impending crisis in their relationship. Jogiches moved to Kraków in Austrian-annexed Poland. (There were frontiers between the three parts of partitioned Poland—Russian, Prussian, and Austrian.) There he organized and supervised the publication of the SDKPiL organ *The Red Banner* and another, *From the Battlefield,* of which he was editor in chief. He also orchestrated the smuggling and distribution of the illegal literature into Russian-annexed Poland. A frequent though illicit guest in Warsaw, he mobilized the party forces: the SDKPiL membership grew dramatically from 200 in 1893 to 30,000 in 1906. After five years of forced inactivity, Jogiches was in his element, jealously guarding his own battlefield from Luxemburg's interference. Impatient, irritated words kept reaching him from Berlin: "What, in fact, are you doing in Kraków?" Luxemburg inquired (April 30). "Don't you really have a minute to write to me . . ." (May 4). "Why the hell don't I know what's going on in Poland and in Kraków?!" (June 28). Her entreaties remained unanswered.

The 1905 revolution exposed the gap between Luxemburg and the German Social Democrats, the gap between being revolutionary and merely theorizing. It appeared unbridgeable. Luxemburg's rather rhetorical question, "When will you finally learn from the Russian revolution?" was little short of a slap in the face to the Germans, who had no intention of learning anything from the "Asiatics." While she conceived of revolution as historical necessity, the SPD saw it as a philosophical, abstract issue. The isolation in which she would play out her final act—the founding of the German Communist Party—was closing in on her.

Nor did her personal life bring solace. A surprise visit she paid Jogiches in Kraków, in August 1905, ended in his angrily reproaching her that she was treating him to "offal," even though trying to "smooth" things out. A man whom Luxemburg refers to as W. (letter 62) appeared in her life, perhaps only in her desperate effort to shake Jogiches up. He indeed came to Berlin in September to straighten things out, but the split that became final in 1907 had been triggered. Until December 1905 when she joined Jogiches in Warsaw, Luxemburg never stopped imploring him to forget the past, to live with the present, to stop despairing.

In March 1906, Luxemburg and Jogiches were arrested by the czarist police in a pension owned by Countess Walewska, where they were staying under false names. Luxemburg was released on bail in June and, after spending three months in Finland (in frequent touch with Lenin), went home to Berlin in the fall of 1906. When Jogiches, sentenced to eight years of hard labor, escaped and returned to that home in April 1907, he learned from her that it was no longer his.

1. Róża Luksemburg, *Wybór Pism* (Warsaw: Książka i Wiedza, 1959), vol. I, pp. 340–345.

"Never before had there been such crowds at a meeting. . . ."

"My success and the public recognition I am getting are likely to poison our relationship. . . ."

Luxemburg at the Congress of the Socialist International, Amsterdam, 1904

Luxemburg at the Congress of the Socialist International, Stuttgart, 1907

Letter 43

[Mainz]
Friday night
[September 21, 1900]

My only, beloved, golden one!

At last I can drop you a few lines. The [SPD] party congress ended today at noon. After an early dinner I had to go on a cruise on the Rhine, so I just got back to the hotel.

You must know from the papers that the debate on customs policy kept me very busy. Calwer's speech was a real scandal![1] I had to talk right after him and without any preparation, but out of sheer rage I spoke very well. I had to talk again after Vollmar, who clearly avoided tangling with me.[2] Vollmar's main motion was finally rejected, and all my motions were accepted. According to Bebel and others, Vollmar is furious. Then a migraine kept me in bed all of Thursday and today till noon so that I couldn't participate in the debate on local elections. It didn't make too bad an impression though. I voted with Singer,[3] Ledebour, and the Berliners.

By and large, our movement can be *very* pleased with the party congress.

1. Our victory in the debate on international politics is unquestionable; Singer himself had to admit it.
2. Needless to say, we won in the customs policy debate.
3. We obtained two additional seats for Berlin in the executive committee!

I myself really benefited enormously. I was the only one who consistently supported our policy. Singer is ecstatic about me. Many delegates thanked me for eating Calwer alive and for my stand on international politics. [. . .] I was asked to speak in big cities all over Germany, the most important invitations coming from Frankfurt am Main, Mainz, Fürth, Nurnberg, in other words, from *southern* Germany, and also from Bochum. [. . .] Eisner told me at dinner that I had mastered the

German language perfectly (Herzfeld agreed) and that as far as style goes I was the best speaker at the congress!! Coming from him it is the highest praise. Finally, my relationship with Auer is sugar-sweet. Tomorrow we're all going to Paris together, where I'm going to play Auer's "mother-in-law." The whole time I stayed close to Clara [Zetkin], and we'll stick together in Paris too.

My Paris speech isn't ready yet, but I've the whole of Sunday to prepare it. [. . .] My migraine's gone, and I'll be fine for the trip tomorrow, I hope. My beloved, my golden one, I'll write you on the way and also from Paris.

I kiss you a thousand times. Everything's all right. Do be pleased with me.

Yours R.

Bebel and others call me "the conqueror" (concerning customs policy). I didn't raise the Bavarian issue *on purpose*. Write to Paris c/o Wladek [Olszewski], 47, rue Beaumier, in two envelopes!

1. Richard Calwer (Calver), an economist and a leading, ultimately right-wing SPD member.
2. Georg von Vollmar, one of the leaders of the right wing in the SPD.
3. Paul Singer, one of the leaders and organizers of German social democrats.

Postcard 44

[Bydgoszcz]
[June 9, 1901]

Everything worked out fine—my resolution was unanimously adopted.[1] Settled things with Śremski too. Moved out of the hotel—it was filthy—into another one. Will be back on Tuesday. Bye for now.

1. The Second Congress of the SPD, Poznań district, was held in Bydgoszcz.

Postcard 45

Rawicz.
Before the meeting.
[June 25, 1901]

Corrected the report for *Volkswacht*, wrote to Zas[ulich?][1] and came here. Will go to Wrocław tomorrow, not to Berlin, because the comrades want me back here for another day. You've no idea how they love me. The meeting was really impressive. I'm very tired but will somehow stick it out for another three days, then on to feed chickens in Jakimówki [a village?].

Yours

1. Vera Zasulich (1851–1919), Russian revolutionary, member of *Zemlya i Volya*, the organizing center of the Populist movement. In 1878 she shot at General Trepov, governor of St. Petersburg. Tried and acquitted by jury, she fled abroad. With the eminent Marxists, Georgii V. Plekhanov and Pavel Akselrod, she founded the "Liberation of Labor" society to propagate Marxism in Russia. From 1900 she collaborated with Lenin in editing *Iskra*, and after the 1903 split joined the Mensheviks. *Iskra* (The Spark), an organ of the Russian Social-Democratic Workers' Party, was founded abroad by Lenin in 1900. After 1903, until its publication ceased in 1905, it was a Menshevik paper.

Letter 46

No. 1 [Berlin]
January 6, 1902

My Dear! I got your letter No. 1 yesterday. From now on I'll number my letters as you asked. What you wrote about the doctor's verdict hit me like a sledgehammer. I've put great hope into Algeria, and even now I think that the difference between the local doctor's prognosis and [doctor] Senator's has to do with the strain of the trip and undernourishment.[1] One comfortable week and his [Józef Jogiches] condition may very well improve. I'm anxiously waiting for further news. [Doctor] Senator clearly and definitely talked in terms of *years*! He's trustworthy, isn't he?

Anyway, try to keep the poor soul believing that food can save him and let him eat to his heart's content. It's the last resort, plus the air and sun. How often is he going to see the doctor? In one of my letters that got lost on its way to you in Nervi, I think I told you about a similar case. I also heard from Kautsky that his brother had had TB, and they *had given him up,* but he recovered in the south (in Bozen, in south Tirol) and now is in Vienna alive and well. So you see, there are many more cases like this than you'd think.

Didn't I write you about poor Potresov? And also there's Dietzgen—he's your brother's age. They put him back on his feet in Italy and then he went safely back to America—here he had been laid up in a hotel with an unremitting fever! I, for one, won't lose hope!

What you say about "the fury" you feel because one more disaster fell tumbling down on top of all your other ordeals—if you'll excuse me my dear (as my sister-in-law says)—is something I can't follow. It's a statement worded in the Sanskrit of your psychology that I so often fail to understand. To my simpleton's mind your mother's death and your brother's tragedy are the only real disasters that deserve compassion and respect. Your constant complaints, "I'm fed up with everything," "it bores the hell out of me," are symptoms of a senseless, savage spiritual suicide, just as your brother's behavior was a symptom of a physical suicide. It is the same self-destructive streak; it gnaws at the roots of existence without reason or purpose. Indeed, the mere sight of it can drive one mad. If you feel impotent with rage watching your brother waste away because he has thoughtlessly savaged his own body, think how I

feel. Think how furious I am day in day out, year after year.
Helplessly, I watch you do the same thing to your soul. You,
too, are wasting yourself. There is no reason but the same savage madness.

You'll be angry that I'm writing about this now when you're
so worried, but you know I'm no diplomat, and, when the
heart is full, the mouth must speak. [. . .]

Everything's fine here at home except that the never-ending
music coming from nearby buzzes in my ears all day long.
Even now I barely know what I'm writing with Chopin rocking
me to sleep hour after hour. I'm anxiously waiting for news
about your brother. Why do you write so late at night? Don't
you have time during the day? Do you have to stay up so late?
Haven't I begged you to go to bed early!! Hugs.

Yours R.

The post office forwarded a registered letter for you to
Algiers which they refused to give to me.

Tell me at last what you want me to do with the letters from
your brother? Destroy them? Mail them to you? They're here,
unopened of course. The postage will cost a fortune, and
there's certainly nothing important in them.

1. J. went to Algeria with his tubercular brother, Józef (Osip), who
died there two months later.

Letter 47

No. 8 [Berlin]
January 20, 1902

My Dear! [. . .] Yesterday I had the three Kautskys over, the
Eisners, and Stadthagen who, naturally, arrived after 9 P.M.,
when we were about to finish dinner. The table looked wonderful (even small bunches of flowers at every plate, 10 pfen-

nig each, and a potted hyacinth in the center). The dishes
were served without a mishap. First, rolls with caviar (don't
faint, 50 pf only), salmon and eggs, followed by borsch with
sausage-stuffed rolls, fish in sour sauce, steak with vegetables,
compote, dessert, cheese with radishes, and black coffee with
cognac. Beverages: beer and lemonade. They teased me with
each new dish, especially Eisner, but devoured everything and
at the end unanimously requested champagne. I went to the
kitchen and brought out the bottle your brother sent, and they
made silly faces. Naturally they emptied the bottle. We sent
Singer a rather dreadful picture postcard, which everybody
signed. They stayed till 1:30 A.M. Mrs. Eisner brought me a
colored photo of her whole family in a beautiful gold frame. I
put it on the little table, where it looks perfect. Now I'm getting back to work. Big hug.

Yours R.

We're negotiating with Warski about the paper. The first issue will have a minimum of four sheets almost the same size
as N[eue] Z[eit]. What topics would you suggest?

Don't miss Potresov's article "The Vestal" in *Zaria*. To my
mind this is the only article written in good Russian, not in the
international Marxist jargon. It is a bit vague but what passion!
It stirred me.

[*not in chronological order*]

[Berlin]
February 13, 1902

[. . .] Your critical comments about the radishes on my
menu "if you'll excuse me, my dear," miss the point. Yes,
here in Germany radishes are served only with cheese, *after*
dinner. Don't be a smart aleck. [. . .]

Letter 48

No. 14 [Berlin]
Tuesday
January 28, 1902

My Dear! Today I got your letter No. 13, dated Friday. Went to the meeting last night. I thought [Clara] Zetkin's speech all right, though not terribly good. The resolution I composed was adopted unanimously. I'll send it to Dubreuilh, it'll make him happy.[1] Poor Clara was exhausted. She forgot a lot of facts and didn't mention me, though she quoted passages from my articles word for word. The hall wasn't big, perhaps 500 people (SD), and packed to the rafters. Half the hall, and *comme de raison* the best places in front, were naturally taken by Russians or rather by kikes from Russia—they were sickening to look at.

I had to walk Clara to Reichshallen on Leipzigerstr. since her eyesight is failing (a cataract's forming on the other eye) and she can't walk alone at night. She had an appointment with [Emmy] Stock.[2] Stock, along with the "crème" of the party, attended a meeting of *Frauen und Mädchen* where Clara Müller, that poet whom I'd met at the Mehrings and who talks with a terrible lisp, recited her poetry. So we found the whole "court" in Reichshallen: the Auers, the Gradnauers,[3] the Eisners, Stadthagen, etc., etc. I wanted to leave at once, but they wouldn't let me go, insisting we walk home together.

They all teased me about my "six course" dinners! What a bunch of gossips! Imagine paying attention to such trivia! N.B. The Eisners and the Gradnauers are most assiduously dancing attendance on me.

Next Sunday I'm going to the Eisners with Clara, the same night that we're invited to the K[autskys'], who are having the Bebels over too. I'll try to excuse myself but will have to go at night to pick up Clara, who wants to sleep at my place.

I'll ask Ledebour to come over that Sunday morning because

I suggested that Clara give him Lili's [Braun] book for review in [*The*] *Gleichheit*.[4] Since Clara wants to lunch with me and go to the Eisners with me later on, I'll probably have Ledebour stay for lunch, too. As you see, because of Clara, I got more involved in the party whirl. This won't last, and it has some advantages too.

As for Singer, you're dead wrong. He was almost in tears in front of Kautsky (whom he met at the Heymans') because he couldn't come to me for dinner. I read in *Vorwärts* that he was indeed speaking [that night] in his electoral district.

I was quite amused by your comments about the tasks and the mission of our Polish paper. How can one be such a dreamer! And all on account of one small illegal paper that is now in Marchlewski's hands! And here you are, talking about spiritual leadership in the Polish society, about decisive influence on the press under all three invaders, etc., etc. Such a serious person talking such nonsense! . . . I'm well aware of the existence of those ideals, just as I'm well aware that we should try to do our best with this paper. But you're dreaming—that African sun must be getting to you. ("You fantast, you . . .")

I went carefully over the issues you sent of *Petite République*. I already had some from K[autsky] and marked them myself, but some you marked will be very useful.

I don't have any intention of meddling in the Krichevsky affair. Bebel has decided to reprint *Zaria's* answer in *Vorwärts,* and in response to my suggestion Clara took a few swipes at Krichevsky in her speech yesterday. She also asked the *Vorwärts* reporter to show her his report of her speech to make sure nothing was hushed up.

I must stop because Anna [the maid] is waiting to take the letter to the post office.

My best to your brother! Hugs.

Yours R.

1. Louis Dubreuilh, French socialist and journalist.
2. Emmy Stock, first head of the working-women's organization "Verein für Frauen und Mädchen der Arbeiterklasse," founded under the auspices of the SPD.
3. Georg Gradnauer, right-wing SPD member, on the editorial board of *Sächsische Arbeiterzeitung* and later of *Vorwärts*.
4. Lili Braun, prominent in the SPD women's movement, writer and author of *Memoiren einer Sozialistin*.

Letter 49

No. 20 [Berlin]
February 11, 1902

My dear Dyodyu! [. . .] As usual, there were some funny moments on the tour. In Reichenbach, after the meeting (in each town one must talk with a few comrades afterward, till 2 A.M., which I don't mind)—well, in Reichenbach one of the local bigwigs kept staring at me. Finally he spoke up, "You can't be more than twenty-seven years old and I thought you were forty-two." "Why?" I asked, surprised. "Well, from your picture in *Süddeutscher Postillon*." You can imagine how I laughed. They'd obviously mistaken the caricature in the paper for a real picture, and each and everyone had loyally kept a copy of it.

For a change, after the meeting in Meerane I was stringently questioned about women's rights and marriage. A splendid, young weaver named Hoffman, has been eagerly pursuing the question, reading Bebel, Lili Braun, and [The] *Gleichheit*. He's been arguing tooth and nail with the older comrades, who insist women belong in the home and want us to fight for the abolition of factory work for women. When I agreed with him, Hoffman was triumphant! "You see," he shouted, "authority supports me!" When one of the older men said it was a shame for a pregnant woman to work among young men in a factory, Hoffman cried: "These are perverse moral concepts! Mind you, if our Luxemburg were pregnant delivering her speech today, I'd have liked her even better!'' I felt like laughing at this unexpected *dictum,* but they all took it so seriously that I had to bite my lip.

Anyhow, I'll have to do everything I can to be pregnant by the next time I come back to Reichenbach. Understand? Before we parted (at 2 A.M.), the young fellow stopped me. He wanted my opinion on an important matter: should he get married even though today marriage is a hypocritical institution? Luckily I said ''yes'' and my answer clearly made him happy. From the smiles and whispers and later from his own admission, it became apparent that he's about to get married. It's about time, too. His fiancée is already in the condition he likes so much. [. . .]

Lots of people joined the unions and subscribed to the party papers at the meetings. The whole trip has been spiritually refreshing though physically tiring. I visited the local weaving school in Glauchau. The foreman was very polite and showed me around. I learned a lot of interesting things. Must stop and write to Clara and to Mehring! Hugs!

Yours R.

Letter 50

No. 25 [Berlin]
February 21, 1902

My dear Dyodyu! Busy day yesterday and I didn't get to write you. Today is Anna's wash day so I did the cooking and cleaning. This afternoon I walked in the sun for an hour, and the brisk air left me so exhausted I'm afraid to start this letter; there's so much I have to tell you.

First, business. Your letter No. 26, dated the 15th and asking for Grandulen [medicine], just arrived today. It's too late now, but I'll definitely take care of it tomorrow.

And now *in medias res*! What a pity you aren't here! We

could sit down on the sofa and talk in peace. This tiresome
scribbling! Well, last night I came home from my brother's at
8 P.M. and found a letter from Mehring delivered by their
housemaid.[1] It read: "Dear Rakowski! Please come immediately, comrades from Leipzig are here. The matter is settled.
Hurrah! Yours F. M."[2] Of course I had to go to Steglitz [a section of Berlin] and run into Mehring, Kleeman, and Beyer
(Press Commission), who were already on the lookout for me.
Apparently they had been waiting for me at Mehring's since
six o'clock (they didn't have my address). We went to a pub
(the fellows were leaving for Leipzig at 11 P.M.) where they
announced they want me for *L[eipziger] V[olkszeitung]*, since
the other suggested candidates were "not [good enough] for
Leipzig."

This is the way they want to proceed: First the Press Commission will formally invite me to become a regular contributor,[3] and then we'll make arrangements for my moving to
Leipzig. They promptly added, any obstacles, like my lease,
"Leipzig can afford to take care of" (obviously they had discussed all details with Mehring). Mehring presided, beaming
with happiness, for he considered the matter settled. But I,
caught unawares with no time to think it over, made a quick
mental calculation and said: "I'll answer you briefly. *At this
point* your offer is limited to asking me to contribute to
Leipziger Volkszeitung, isn't it? I've no reason to turn it down.
I'm ready to cooperate, particulars subject to discussion. Concerning your further plans—my moving to Leipzig and taking
over the editorship—it's no simple matter, and I can't give you
a *definite* answer now. We'll see."

They agreed, of course repeating along with Mehring that
there's no other solution and that's that. I didn't argue, first,
because I had no idea what decision to make and anyway
couldn't say anything *definite* without consulting you; second,
because it was a preliminary discussion. Indeed, even to become a contributor requires an official invitation from the

Press Commission, which they'll extend by the *second half of March* (I pressed for the late date). The Commission will invite me to deliver a lecture at an open meeting, convene their assembly at the same time and invite me to the session. The Mehrings will go to Leipzig with me (! they're simply mad with joy).

That's it. As you see, life refuses to grant us a little peace. Something always happens that turns our life upside down. But this time it's a moment of *great significance* requiring careful consideration before saying yes or no.

I don't have to make a formal decision at the March conference either, since only my collaboration will be discussed there. But on the other hand both the Leipzig people and Mehring understand my collaboration in terms of my immediate support of the paper with the editorship to follow. To stall too long would be out of place, and Mehring would never forgive me. Even though I won't give them a definite answer in March, in Leipzig, *I myself* at least must know what I want because inner hesitation always shows and inspires mistrust and lack of respect. It's imperative that I discuss it with you immediately (considering the snail's pace of our correspondence), so I can have your definite opinion before I go to Leipzig.

In fact, we both know all the pros and cons, and the whole point is what outweighs what. Still, I feel it my duty to give you a comprehensive though concise picture of the situation, so that nothing escapes your attention.

First, what makes both of us shudder instantly is the fear of a new upheaval, of wrecking the quiet haven we've just built and haven't even started to enjoy, of leaving the pleasant apartment in the quiet Friedenau. In other words a change, an upheaval, a strain, while we both crave peace!!! Every word you may write on this point is needless because you can't possibly crave peace more than I do. So let's make a long story short and look at the question from a different angle:

First of all, it's out of the question to move to Leipzig *immediately*. Under no circumstances will I agree to move before October so that when you come back we can enjoy a quiet summer and a vacation. Next, the sense of hope and security we feel now comes from having, at long last, *our own apartment and our own household*. Naturally we'll have this in Leipzig too. The present situation won't even be remotely similar to that in Dresden.[4] No more of this crazy nonsense, living in hotels, etc. Never again. In a purely German fashion we'll take our time, find a suitable apartment in Leipzig somewhere in the villa section near the woods (Leipzig has magnificent woods), then we'll slowly pack our furniture (of course we'll have the party cover the moving expenses), and take Anna [the maid] with us. In short, taking our time, without stress or strain, we'll make arrangements and settle down in a truly middle-class fashion, and it will be all done *before* I take over the editorship. And we'll live exactly as we do here and we'll cook the same "apple soup," which you recall with such relish. (Nota bene, you ungrateful piglet, why do you write "if not tomato soup, then 'at least' apple soup!" Haven't you stuffed yourself, if you'll pardon the expression, many times with tomato soup!!)

Surely you must know one can live in Leipzig as quietly and delightfully as in Friedenau. Moreover there are no Kautskys and no Neufelds there; there's no one. Schönlank didn't know a single soul because there's no party intelligentsia there, just common workers. Anyway, not a single soul knows us there, and, since I'm not going to entertain, our relationship will escape attention (we'll have to be a little cautious only when we go to town together). Also, there's an excellent theater where we can go often and for free, excellent concerts, and to top it all off, a five to six weeks' summer vacation yearly.

And now the second point. In addition to the external upheaval, there'll be hard work, responsibility, in short, *inner* unrest. The answer to this: these matters too look entirely differ-

ent now than four years ago in Dresden. Then I didn't have
the remotest knowledge of the bourgeois press, and I was unfamiliar with *Kreuzzeitung* (in fact its name is different). I had
only a very vague idea about the technique of running a newspaper. Today I'm at home with the bourgeois press and don't
feel as I did in Dresden, as if I were setting out on uncharted
seas in a derelict boat.

Moreover, please take into consideration that *L[eipziger]
V[olkszeitung]* is technically so well organized and on such a
high level that I don't have to introduce any reforms, as I had
to in *S[ächsische] A[rbeiterzeitung]*. No need to improve the
form; the contents—decent articles and stories—are the only
concern. Here I can count on Mehring. Now he'll be devoted
to the paper body and soul and will help me out where I'm
weak: Prussian history, Prussian politics, academic life, party
history, etc. I myself will concentrate mainly on the party *line*
and party *politics*. *Cunow,* anxious to work and producing like
a machine, may be attracted because of Mehring, possibly also
Schippel, and a few Frenchmen. So, relatively speaking, I
won't have that much work. Besides, *Jaeckh* will stay on, and
Mehring says he's an efficient writer.

Now what does this affair *bring* us? First: loads of money.
We could live care-free, spend summers in Switzerland or at
the seaside, dress decently, buy things for the apartment (help
our folks—this is *my* special concern, and as you know I've
Andzia [sister] in mind), save several hundred marks every
month.

Second and most important: *A political position.* You know
yourself what it means to be editor in chief of the leading
party paper. You also know that the old fogies and *all* the rest,
the Bavarians, the foreigners, will immediately look at me differently, aware that I hold such a powerful weapon in my
hand. And most important, the *position*; a permanent position
that *is there every day,* not one to be secured by yet another
effort, by yet another article.

Third: Life and work regulated by an outer structure, instead of each morning starting with the nebulous question of where to begin, what to write, what to reach for. I think an external framework that provides stability and order will sooth and heal our nerves better than anything else could. Your letters prove that what you want and need is not an idle, aimless peace, but peace through struggle and work, stable and regular. In spite of all the misery around you and in spite of your yearning for tranquillity, you only feel alive when you hear the sound of battle trumpets, the sound of work and struggle. There is no work more *stable* and peaceful, not in the whole world I daresay, than editorial work.

One more thing. You might answer maliciously, "If you recommend order and regularity in life so eagerly, why haven't you managed to introduce some into yours?" Well, here you're wrong, dead wrong! Ever since I've had my own home and my own household, we've been living with clockwork order and precision. Every penny spent is accounted for, every matter promptly taken care of, every letter promptly answered. I run a taut ship—the cooking, washing, cleaning, the clothes and linen, the books and pamphlets and newspapers are in perfect order. In short, it is impossible to live a more regular life and woe unto you when you come back. I've set up the way we're going to live, and you'd better fit meekly into the routine of our household.

If I still haven't managed to do much work, don't forget that after you left I was a complete nervous wreck, and it took several weeks before I pulled myself together. Undefined work, poor relations with *Neue Zeit,* the lack of stimulus that had been provided by *Leipziger Volkszeitung* don't make things easier. You know best how much I need a goad in order to work efficiently.

One more point. You wrote once, when Mehring wanted to help me [to get a job], that you'd surely *oppose* it because you've learned to look at things more calmly, to follow the example of the Germans who, like Mehring, turn down excellent jobs for the most trifling personal reasons. Well, first of all, Mehring officially turned down the job because "his wife would have no social life in Leipzig." To *me* he confessed the whole truth: he didn't expect to gain prestige or a higher position and, in fact, he was rather afraid of losing prestige in the new experiment because he'd actually never been an editor nor does he have a knack for editing; as a matter of fact, he only wrote editorials in the [*Berliner*] *Volkszeitung* when the paper was run by others. So you see that before he rejected this plum, Mehring had given it a lot of thought and was guided by the pure and simple reason that while he didn't have much to gain he had a lot to lose. I am in exactly the opposite situation—I can hardly lose any fame, but I can gain it simply *by being* editor in chief.

Moreover, if we have both learned to take things more calmly and without exaggeration, my work as editor should profit by it. Instead of killing ourselves, instead of trying to start out with epoch-making articles, we'll pursue our goal calmly and persistently.

Finally, let me say this. While assessing the problem, disregard all considerations such as why Blos was their first choice, why they didn't come straight to me, why this or that. Such backstage trifles vanish without a trace. What remains is *the hard fact*: who is in charge of the leading party paper. It would indeed be grotesque if such whims prompted a decision that could determine our life for many *years*.

Dyodyu, I emphasized the *pros* not to force your agreement but simply because it is your natural inclination to stress the *cons*.[5] However, I hope that at a time as important as this (remember, it is a chance of a lifetime! I tried my luck, as it were, with *S*[*ächsische*] *A*[*rbeiterzeitung*] and *Vorwärts,* and *N*[*eue*] *Z*[*eit*]), you'll rid yourself of your inherent reluctance to take a bold step (you'll be angry with me for saying this;

I've already got goose pimples), and your natural inclination to rear up in fear at an important moment.

Consider the *pros* and *cons* soberly (would you like me to send you Askev's booklet *Pros and Cons?*) and write me what you think. I've made no decision yet, but you well know I wouldn't do anything *against* your will.

Mehring walked with me in Friedenau till 12:30 A.M., clasped my hands, mad with joy. It tickles him to imagine the expression on the faces of the oldtimers when they hear the news![6] Of course, I asked him to keep it secret and reminded him that I haven't made up my mind. The Mehrings have already announced they'll come and visit me every month when I settle in Leipzig, and so will Clara [Zetkin] every time she's in Berlin. (A nice prospect!)

Tomorrow night I must go and see the Mehrings. He called after me, "Please don't forget your door key."

This is a whole lot of scribbling, all for you, and I'm exhausted but *saturavi animam meam.* [I have satisfied my soul.]

Dyodyo, my dearest, I want so much to make your life happy!

1. L.'s brother, Maksymilian (Munio), was living temporarily in Berlin.
2. Rakowski, a joking nickname made up by F. Mehring.
3. Every large city in Germany had its own social democratic newspaper. On the orders of the SPD, each newspaper was supervised by a press commission.
4. L. refers to living in Dresden in 1898 when she was editor in chief of *Sächsische Arbeiterzeitung.*
5. It was L.'s experience that J. was dead set against her taking a permanent job. When she was offered the editorship of *Sächsische Arbeiterzeitung,* he cabled, "unconditionally decline." In 1899 she was offered an editorial post with *Leipziger Volkszeitung;* on August 25 she wrote to J., ". . . my decision to accept the job in Leipzig is almost final. . . ," only to turn down the job two days later. J. claimed that a permanent job was bound to ruin her scholarly and political future (letter 31).
6. The editorship did not materialize. A contemporary member of the *Leipziger Volkszeitung* editorial board, Friedrich Stampfer, of-

fered the following advice to F. Mehring: ". . . es wäre notwendig sein, aufzupassen, dass sie (Luxemburg) in der Parteipolemik nicht über die Stränge schlage. . ." [it will be necessary to watch out, that she (Luxemburg) doesn't go overboard in party polemics]. F. Stampfer, *Erfahrungen und Erkenntnisse* (Cologne: Verlag für Politik und Wirtschaft, 1957), p. 72.

Postcard 51

[Bydgoszcz]
Thursday
[May 28, 1903]

My treasure!

Yesterday's meeting was superb. There were 1500 people crowded in the hall and under the windows! It was filled to the rafters. The local papers had trumpeted my arrival, "the known leader of the SD—R. L. will speak in Tivoli," so the bourgeoisie came trooping in. My lecture went splendidly, and the audience was tremendously excited. The movement is really flourishing here.

Today I'm going to a big meeting in Trzcianka. I told Kasprzak to get directly in touch with you; everything you yourself wrote me in connection with those affairs is complete nonsense so I merely shrug my shoulders. You people can do whatever you please; I don't have the time now to write about it. Letters will be coming for me from Berlin and from here. Keep them. See you Saturday. Hugs.

Yours R.

Postcard 52

[Piła]
[May 29, 1903]

My treasure!

I'm sitting in Piła (Schneidemühl) now, waiting for a train to

Chodzież (Colmar). Yesterday's meeting in Schoenlanke
[Trzcianka] was extremely beautiful. The "concert hall" was
full, at least 500 people, among them, of course, the entire
Jewish bourgeoisie. The local comrades said they had never
had such a full house. Gogowski, as a candidate, spoke, or
rather whined, after me, and he ended his speech using the
municipal slaughterhouses as an example of how socialism
could work. . . . Today we'll both talk in Chodzież and tomorrow I'll be in Berlin. Have Anna wait for me at the train,
otherwise I'll have to take a droshky with all my luggage. The
heat is unbearable. I expect that a letter from Gerisch with further instructions will be waiting for me at home.[1] I'll probably
stay in Berlin three whole days. Hugs.

Yours R.

I'll probably arrive at 11:28 A.M. at Friedrichstr. If the time
changes I'll wire today. Have Anna wait at the station at
11:30.

1. K. A. Gerisch, under the pen name A. Ger, wrote novels about
the life of German workers, which enjoyed considerable success.
He was a metal worker and member of the executive committee of
the SPD.

Postcard 53

[Glauchau]
[June 10, 1903]

My Dear! Again I couldn't write to you yesterday after the
meeting because I had to hurry to Glauchau and it was already past midnight. Yesterday's meeting in Oberlungwitz was
fabulous. People said that never before had there been such
crowds at a meeting. I heard there had been a meeting here in
1898 at which Auer spoke, and 45 people showed up. Yester-

day some 900 came. Tremendous excitement, they welcomed me, bade farewell with cheers, and saw me off at the station. Today I have the last meeting in support of Auer. I met Gradnauer here this morning! He had a meeting last night, went to Leipzig today. We really enjoyed meeting each other. I feel rather shaky, though I speak with vigor, and Gr[adnauer] was surprised I look so *frisch.* I received *Berliner Tageblatt.* Hugs.

Yours R.

Postcard 54

[Hamburg]
[June 24, 1903]

My Dear! Yesterday I didn't have the time to write after the meeting, which went on till 11:30 P.M. Then I had to hurry, catch the electric [train], and get back to the hotel in Hamburg.

The meeting in Wilhelmsburg was superb, jam-packed. It was difficult to speak, still I talked for two full hours with tremendous success. There were many people from Hamburg and the editor of *The Harburger V*[olksblatt], from Harburg, etc. Many thanks and no end of congratulations. Today I have a Polish meeting in Wilhelmsburg. There's no doubt the district is lost to us because the work is badly managed; the Hamburgers have let it slip completely.

I didn't write anything for the paper yesterday because, after getting back, I lay down to take a nap and woke up at 7 P.M.! But at least I felt refreshed at the meeting. Today I'm putting it all into one article. Am well but have a headache. Will be back tomorrow. See you soon.

R.

Postcard 55

                                    [Dresden]
                                    [September 19, 1903]

My treasure!

Am dog tired. The debate about tactics ended today. *I didn't get to speak* but don't care. Tomorrow the congress will continue,[1] the day after tomorrow I must appear in court; was summoned, no one understands why, probably a mistake. They must be mistaking me for Clara [Zetkin]. I will wire what happens, don't worry, I talked it over with Bebel. On the whole I'm in high spirits and cheerful.

Don't worry about anything, everything'll be all right! Clara, alas, is coming back with me!

                                    Hundreds of kisses!
                                    Yours R.

1. The SPD party congress in Dresden.

Letter 56

[*original in German*]
[*Note: Because of prison censorship L. addressed J. as a woman friend; his name Leo became Leonie.*]

                                    [Prison in Zwickau][1] Friday
                                    [September 9, 1904]
                                    Two weeks exactly, so 1/6 is
                                    over!

My dearest Leonie! Do me a couple of favors—it's urgent. I need a warmer blouse—it's high time you got me one. I'm wearing the zephyr blouse, but it's filthy and it's a pity to ruin the gray mousseline here. Strange how soon clothes wear out here, much sooner than at home, though I don't do a thing and hardly move. Lili [sister-in-law] promised me a skirt (the navy blue skirt is worn out and the black one with the royal train isn't exactly appropriate for a cell!). Józio [Józef, brother] came to see me and will remind Lili, so I should get the skirt soon. I won't need the *hat* till I leave prison (26 October, 11 A.M.) because I just walk in the yard, hatless. Get a size 44 blouse, the simpler the better and not in a striking color. Munio [Maksymilian, brother] sent the warden 100 M from Warsaw for my own food, but I didn't accept it because Dietz provides all I need.[2] I was sorry I had a migraine and didn't look well when Józio visited. Usually I feel fine.

The second urgent favor: please give the second part of this letter to Karl [Kautsky] immediately.[3] [. . .]

You want to know everything about me. Here it is: I get up at 6 A.M., get coffee at 7, walk from 8 to 9, lunch at 12, at 3 have coffee, at 6 supper, from 7 to 9 lamplight, at 9 bed. I get *Berliner Tageblatt.* I read a lot and think a great deal. What is Warski doing? Have him write to me. I hope you took care of the paper I promised the Kreuzbergers. Have Warski send my address to Clara [Zetkin]. I want to hear from her.

Best regards.
Yours R.

When I left, you promised you'd read one book a day. Do you? You *must,* I beg you! Now I appreciate again the value of making serious books a part of daily life. It saves the mind and the *nervous* system. But Marx, you know, ends up by making me angry. I still *can't get the better* of him. I keep getting swamped and can't catch my breath.

What is Parvus doing? Give him my regards. Write to him, don't leave him alone.

Please send me promptly the German edition of *The Communist Manifesto* and *The Divine Comedy* in German (we have it, published by Reclam).

Why don't you send me some stockings (the smallest woman's size), but have them washed because new ones stain the feet. Three pairs would be fine.

I hope you still get up early and go to bed early. I'm happy every time I think how well you've been looking. I attribute this only to your getting up early. But then *why* did Luise [Kautsky] have to ring the doorbell for so long?

1. In 1904 L. was sentenced to three months of prison for insulting the Emperor Wilhelm II in one of her speeches.
2. J. H. W. Dietz was the party publisher (see letter 31, n.1).
3. Last names are not substituted for first names (see letter 2, n.2) to preserve L.'s caution of prison censorship.

Letter 57
[*original in German*]

> [Prison in Zwickau]
> Friday
> September 23, 1904
> (13 − 4 = 9)

My beloved Leonia! To start with, figure out the cabalistic formula above. Many thanks for the parcel. The blouse is excellent. I made some alterations and wear it all the time. The cap, too, made an "interesting topic," didn't it? I wish you wouldn't dwell on these topics like some pedantic spinster, Goldilocks, or I'll lose my patience. When I finally get a letter from outside, there are many things I'd rather hear about than a shopping-for-a-blouse odyssey. I got neither The [Communist] Manifesto nor the clippings attached to Luise's letter (Karl's article). Tell her it's pointless to send them. Of course you could have risked *Kladderadatsch*—I suppose I'd have gotten it.[1] A good joke is my only cure for all worries, and the last issue was just magnificent.

That you live such a lonely life is insane and abnormal, and I take a very dim view of it. My present mood makes me hate such "asceticism" more than ever. Here I keep grasping greedily at each spark of life, each glimmer of light, each nuance in the feuilletons and theater reviews in *Berliner Tageblatt*. I promise myself *to live* life to its fullest as soon as I'm free, and you, you just sit there overflowing with riches and, like Saint Anthony in the desert, live on wild honey and locusts! You'll turn into a barbarian, my dear girl, and when I come out of prison your Nazarene bloodlessness will clash violently with my Hellenic full-bloodedness! "Watch out, Buseli," as Frau Löwe used to say to her little kitten. Remember? It's too bad I can't brandish the rug beater as ominously as she did.

You want me to describe my cell, do you? No small order, *my darling* [orig. Eng.]. Where do I get the brush and watercolors to do justice to these riches! I just noticed a hectographed inventory of my cell on the wall and much to my surprise discovered there are about twenty objects here. And I was convinced the cell was entirely empty! The moral of the story: whoever feels poverty stricken should sit down and make an "inventory" of his earthly possessions, just to discover how rich he is. You should make an inventory of your riches more often, and if you don't forget to include my modest person, as you unfortunately so often do, you will feel like Croesus. [. . .]

> Many, many kisses.
> Yours R.

1. *Kladderadatsch,* a satirical magazine famous for political cartoons, founded in Berlin in 1848.

Letter 58

[original in German]

[Prison in Zwickau]
Tuesday
October 4, 1904

My dear girl! Rejoice, for here's another letter from me to you, written mainly to reassure your heart that is so deeply concerned with my stomach. At my own wish I've given up the restaurant dinners and have gone back to the prison fare. Now I feel fine. My stomach has simply had enough of cultural refinements, and it yearns for Rousseau. So for the last week I've been indulging in vegetarian pleasures, like King Nebuchadnezzar, by divine verdict condemned to crawl on all fours and to eat grass (Heine maintains it was lettuce). Nota bene, I still get a piece of meat each evening. You might as well calm down and forget this topic for good. If only you could stop playing "auntie" altogether, give up the projects of fruit deliveries, the concern for my fleshly delights—things about which, to use Bismarck's kitchen Latin: *Nescio, quod mihi magis farcimentum esset,* or in plain German: *Ich weiss nicht was mir mehr 'Wurscht' wäre!* [I couldn't care less!].

Did you hear me scream last night? Imagine: suddenly I wake up at 2:30 from the deepest sleep, don't know where I am, and in greatest fear I call, of course, for my Mother.[1] My ear-piercing voice can probably be heard in Friedenau! And it takes a full ten minutes till I realize I am calling her seven years too late. You cannot imagine the oppressive feeling that came over me. The night's incident is a shadow that has been following me all day long, and I look at the beautiful sunny day as through a veil. It certainly isn't the fault of my poor cell because the same thing happened to me once in Friedenau, only then my dearest sister sleeping "the sleep of the just" didn't hear anything either. I didn't want to tell you about it later since it was one of the seven days of the week on which we were "parting company."

Now let me ask you for several things: send me Cunow's series of articles about cartels which were published in *Neue Zeit* in the spring, I think. The topic is a hard nut to crack, and in the books I brought with me there is little except rubbish. And these, mind you, are the "most fundamental" books in the field! The whole question is, as it were, fallow ground. . . .

Can I work here? Of course, it's perfectly quiet, only the happy sound of children chattering with a Saxonian lilt comes from somewhere (I've no idea where my window faces), along with the busy quacking of ducks coming, I think, from a pond in a nearby park. Those ducks must all be of the female sex; not for a single hour can they "keep their bills shut." Even in the middle of the night they carry on fervent conversations, their qua-qua descending down the scale with such pathos and conviction that, despite my anger, I always laugh.

I wasn't permitted to get Lavigne's letter.[2] About Karl [Kautsky] and August [Bebel], I had exactly the same thoughts as you. Do go and see Luise [Kautsky], as usual.

You should have talked to Anna [the housemaid]. If I'm to hire her from New Year's, why should the poor girl change jobs twice and mess up her credentials? Perhaps she can stand it till New Year's on her present job?

That will do. Now you can wait a bit longer, for the next letter is going to Warsaw. Let's see if you find "the strength and the stuff" to write to me on your own! . . .

1. This is one of the rare instances when L. speaks of her mother. See also letter 66.
2. Raymond Lavigne, French activist in the labor movement and trade unions.

Letter 59

[Berlin]
Sunday
[May 21, 1905]

Dear One! I just got the proofs this morning, so it was out
of the question to do as you asked and return them "on
Sunday."[1]

I went over the proofs very carefully, so please include all
my corrections and two inserts: (1) about armaments as you
requested, (2) more about the economic struggle. Your supplement to *The Red Banner* is indeed tremendously impressive,
and it gave me ideas for the finishing touches.[2] The issue is
chic. One sees a skilled hand at work since you took over;
everything "clicks" and moves forward smoothly. Still, I don't
agree with you about the factory commissions. You silly jackass, what you lack is "class" instinct; from excessive radical-
ism you slipped straight into opportunism. That happens
when one is radical simply out of a "sense of duty."

Actually the insert belongs in the introduction to the supplement, but this place is just as good. The insert clarifies the first
part of "What Next [?]";[3] otherwise, one could read into it
that the awakening of class consciousness only affects those
mangy apothecaries, clerks, and so on.

As a whole, "What Next [?]" is strikingly impressive but—
but—but—"there's the rub"—I protest most strenuously
against publishing it as a pamphlet. It *must* be a *publication,*
therefore the format of "What Next [?]" must be retained;
only then does it throb with the pulse of revolution. Nor will
the intelligentsia respect a measly little pamphlet, and that's
precisely what you can't grasp, *mein Lieber*. Therefore, I *cate-*
gorically insist that the *format* of "What Next [?]" stays un-
changed. I only give in on the title. Let's call the publication
"From the Revolutionary Era," subtitled "What Next?" No. 2.

Underneath, in *parentheses,* put whatever you want (general strike and economic strike, etc.). I'd like very much to retain the title "What Next [?]" for just *this one time*—it has a ring to it. But finally, I'll give up on *that.* The format, no! Not for the riches of India. You silly jackass.

Still no answer from Marchlewski. He got my letter yesterday morning, so I should have a wire from him announcing his arrival later today.

Do not berate Długi, I beg you.[4] The doctor found his wife in a bad way; that's why he's gone to see her. It's really barbaric to berate him for it! Edda probably won't be able to come here, but then, I swear to god, all she does is get on my nerves.[5] I cannot always be pulling her out of her doldrums, and her nervous look makes me ill in turn. Anyway, everything will go smoothly here, don't worry. It doesn't matter that Długi's going to write his articles from Zurich. As for making some money, I'm doing the best I can. I'll send you [an article] for [*The Red*] *Banner* today/tomorrow. Doesn't look as if there'll be enough space for an article on the French [unification of socialists]. Will send the materials. Witold hasn't sent me anything.[6]

Hugs.

R.

[. . .]

N.B. Don't you dare leave out my motto from Mickiewicz [famous Polish poet], or I'll publicly protest the vandalism of the editors.

1. With the revolutionary wave sweeping over Russia and Poland, J. moved to Kraków (Austrian-annexed Poland) to supervise the editing of the SDKPiL publications. Based in Kraków, he moved illegally between Warsaw and Berlin.
2. *The Red Banner* [*Czerwony Sztandar*], popular journal of the SDKPiL established in 1902 in Zurich, later published in Kraków.
3. In her article "What Next?" L. assessed the 1905 revolution.
4. Mieczysław Dobranicki, member of the SDKPiL.

5. Edda Hirschfeld-Tenenbaum, member of the *Algemener Yid-disher Arbeter Bund* in Łódź, Poland, and later of the SDKPiL. From 1909 to 1911, she was secretary of *Die Gleichheit* editorial board, in the 1920s worked in the Communist International in Moscow, and after 1946 was a member of the Polish Workers' Party.
6. Witold, pseudonym of Władysław Feinstein, member of the Warsaw Committee of the SKDPiL. Since 1921 he had lived in the USSR. He perished in the 1938 purges.

Letter 60

[Berlin]

[May 26, 1905]

My Dear! I'm delighted you've proved your "fallibility" for once. The printing of "What Next?" is an idiot's dream.

1. A supplement to *No. 24* [instead of No. 26] of *The R*[ed] *B*[anner]!! *Mazel tov!*

2. You might as well save the fairy tales for yourself— "nothing could be done" despite some "clever tricks." Sixteen pages make eight columns no matter how you look at it. It was enough to set two pages vertically into one column, and you'd have the supplement without any "clever tricks." (Besides, when I mailed you the manuscript I suggested twelve columns.)

3. It is either/or! If "What Next?" was to be a *supplement* of [*The Red*] *Banner,* it should have had the same format as the newspaper, or, if it was meant to be a *pamphlet,* the inscription "Supplement to [*The Red*] *Banner*" is entirely out of place. I fail to understand this foul business—it's too stupid for words.

4. "What Next?" is fine. But if you retain an old title, to indicate it is a follow-up article, you must call it "What Next?" *No. 2*! Otherwise, the repetition is merely confusing. Also, why have the *subtitles* you suggested disappeared?

5. Don't stick in such stinking prose: *"only by such means*

as among others, for instance, by increasingly intensifying the demonstrations,'' etc. That is simply horrendous. Spare me those cowardly ''ifs and buts,'' and ''more or less''—''such means'' either must be clearly defined or not mentioned at all. Regardless of the abominable style, what's clear in the way you hedge is the ''caution'' of a hesitant man afraid to spell things out—a man who doesn't know what to say himself.

If my style is going to be ''corrected,'' I'm going to stop writing. Why were my ''Cossack figures'' transformed into ''the dreary figures of *absolutism.*'' Who's the idiot who writes about the figures of absolutism? I wonder. Hugs.

R.

My irritation is in fact caused by the *Peuple.*
Marchlewski is here, running after business.

Telegram 61

Berlin
September 17, 1905

DEAR MISSED YESTERDAY'S TELEGRAPH MESSENGER STOP MESSAGE JUST RECEIVED EARLY MORNING TODAY STOP PEOPLE ALL DAY YESTERDAY, KAUTSKY, LUISE, MAN FROM LODZ STOP WAS UNTHINKABLE TO WRITE STOP BE CALM DEAR ALL WILL BE WELL STOP AM UNWAVERING STOP WRITING MORE TODAY SPECIAL DELIVERY STOP THOUSAND GREETINGS STOP PLEASE BE CALM.[1]

1. The telegram and two subsequent letters, which followed J.'s short visit to Berlin, suggest there was a man in L.'s life whom she refers to as W. On August 22 she wrote to J.: ''. . . I didn't understand what you were referring to by the word 'offal' in your postcard and by saying I wanted to 'smooth' things out. . . . You don't want to understand that nothing has changed in my *inner* relationship with you. . . .''

Letter 62

[Berlin]
Sunday morning
[September 17, 1905]*

Dear! I've just wired you urgently. God knows when you'll get it. I almost bit my fingers off when I found your telegram of yesterday under the door. And on top of it, the messenger didn't even ring this morning, just slipped it in. I didn't find it until nine o'clock when the mailman's ringing woke me up (*the charwoman didn't come today*; her week was up yesterday; she's coming back next week).

Dear, my dear, why are you tormenting yourself, why? Now, all we must think of is our task, our work. We need peace, you and I, and all of us.

I'm utterly unwavering in my decisions, as I wired you today, so be calm and think only of the future. Lately, *even yesterday*, I've been going through *an ordeal, an agony,* but now I feel a seed of peace, of silence within me.

W. arrived here aware that the decision had been made, and he didn't say a word to make me change my mind. He wants to move to Kraków for good and should be stopped. Do everything to stop him.

I couldn't wait to write you a few words yesterday but the Kautskys obviously sensed you'd already left when I stopped by at lunch and the avalanche started yesterday morning: he and she, and the children, and Wurm[1] and his wife, and that second German from Łódź—they kept running in and out. Then I had to rush to the washerwoman. After that W. arrived, and on top of it my dreadful monthly pains.

Luise [Kautsky] will pick me up today at 2 P.M. and we'll go together [to the SPD congress in Jena]. I had a letter from Clara [Zetkin]. We'll stay along with the Kautskys in the Hotel Kaiserhof. Write me daily if only a word or two. Aim for the morning or night delivery; I may not be back in the hotel during the day.

That night on the platform a light shone in your window for a long, long time, till the train turned. Deliberately I kept standing in the light of the lamp so that you'd see me. I wanted so badly to be better, more cheerful in those last minutes, and I couldn't, and you looked so ghastly. *Now you must look better again, remember! Be strong, Dyodyu, be strong! Now that the worst is over there'll be only peace and energetic work.* How I need a rest!! As you certainly do.

Dear! Write back at once if you have calmed down. What a nuisance this article about Kasprzak in the midst of all that!

Dear, please be calm, have hope. I embrace you tenderly.

R.

* [*Date written in Jogiches's handwriting. Emphasis added by Jogiches throughout.*]
1. Emanuel Wurm, a prominent SPD activist and journalist. He and his wife Mathilda, herself a writer and journalist and since 1920 a deputy to the Reichstag, belonged to L.'s small circle of personal friends.

Letter 63

[On the way from Berlin to Jena]
[September 17, 1905]

Dear, I'm on my way and you still haven't left Katowice. This waiting's awful. Remember, you cannot make any decisions about yourself without me. We'll think about it together as soon as you've finished with those conferences.

Write to me, please, do. I'll write to you anyway. Your eyes! That look in your eyes!

R.

Letter 64

[Berlin]
[October 10, 1905]

Dear! Today I got your letter in which, after a long-winded opening, you said nothing. Shame on you for criticizing me about Sunday. What do you mean I had nothing to do? Have you forgotten that *la donna* [the maid] arrived Saturday night, so on Sunday I "instructed" her. From early in the morning I showed her how to clean first one room, then another, how to cook, set the table, wash the dishes, make coffee, prepare supper, make the beds, and so on until bedtime. This interesting litany is your punishment. Now you know that I'm not "looking for excuses."

Nota bene, my *Hausfrausorgen* are not over yet. *La donna* is already complaining of palpitations; she cannot climb the stairs, she cannot lift anything. A month, at the utmost, seems all I'll manage to keep her. But I've already "something" in view to replace her so I don't care. Instead I prefer to watch the painter painting figures on the ceiling.

It tears me apart that it's so hard for me to write. Damn it, I can't be a genuine writer after all if I have to pull myself by the hair to force myself to write any old thing. Only under unusual circumstances, like when I get all excited (as when I started on L[eipziger] V[olkszeitung], or during the February revolution), is my pen "winged." And when I'm sweating out an article, I feel so discouraged I can't even write a decent letter and feel like hiding in a dark corner.

Do you know what my bedtime reading is? The autobiography of Benvenuto Cellini in Goethe's translation. An extremely original work, interesting as a mirror of fifteenth-century Italy and France. Gradually I want to get to know my own classics well. Goethe has a soothing effect on me—a genuine "Olympian," I feel such affinity, such closeness with his Weltanschauung. Unfortunately I don't have Goethe's iron industriousness (to say nothing of his genius). The breadth of the universal spiritual interests this man had! It's incredible! And this was a "Hun." I wish somebody would explain this to me. And still, if we read together at night, we won't read fiction but something serious. Life is too short and our ignorance too great to afford such luxury. Agreed? Yes, I got a postcard from Andzia. She's back and well. She found the lilies of the valley still fresh and asked me to thank you. She's very sorry she missed you and expects you during your next visit. Write her a postcard and send it to Złota Street.

Hugs. R.

May I know who this interesting young man is whom I recommended *chaleureusement* to Sigg?[1] Remember, the last thing I need is to get myself into a mess like Clemençeau with his "son". . . .

1. J. Sigg, a leading Swiss social democrat.

Letter 65

[Berlin]
[October] 18 [1905]

My dear Dyodyu! Both your letters came this morning. You mentioned a special delivery letter from me, but I've no idea when I wrote and was sure you wouldn't get anything from me yesterday. My head is like a sieve.

Please read my article very carefully since I sent it off without reading it. I deliberately wrote the paragraph about what it means "to prepare an armed insurrection" so that we won't look like Lenin's *Schildknappen* [henchmen]; Lenin *juxtaposes* it to the participation in the Duma, but what he really means by it is arming oneself.[1] That's why I didn't feel too good about your accepting that clause in the resolution which, in effect, acquired a Bolshevik tinge.

Your far-ranging plans of political agitation in connection with the Duma described in your letter really pleased me. All this is superb and I see I need not worry because you are really *thinking* about the work. The publication of the pamphlet "What do we want [?]" should be part of the battle campaign.[2]

When writing to Vienna, you may refer to my letter and theirs to me.[3] N. B., merely guessing, I've already emphasized in my letter that *their* own delegate had had no reservations about "condemnation" and added that, this being so, they shouldn't bear us a grudge.

As to Parvus allegedly "joining" the Riasanov "group," that is a fairy tale and if spread by the *Iskra* group an impudent one to boot.[4] What a face Parvus would make if he knew about it! N. B. Trotsky is (in P[etersburg]) against *Iskra,* but at the same time is supporting some other ficticious elections.[5]

Afternoon. Your third letter just came. I'd like you to write a clever letter to the *Iskra* group saying how you defended them. I expect you at least told Klim.[6]

Riasanov knows you'll be coming here soon and he is waiting patiently. I don't remember whether I mentioned to him that you'd been here, but in any case he paid no attention to it and everything's all right.

In view of your plans regarding the Duma, I'm glad I wrote a mile-long article, though you may be annoyed that the printing of *From the Battlefield* will take longer, and the issue will be bigger.[7] [. . .]

> I embrace you. Write.
> Yours R.

1. In L.'s view "preparation for the people's revolt" must be achieved by raising the consciousness of the workers and "not by

discussing how to arm the masses, how to provide weapons, or organize 'fighting squads.'" Rosa Luxemburg, "To arms against 'the constitution' of the knout!" in *Z Pola Walki* [*From the Battlefield*], October 18, 1905.

2. "What do we want? Comments on the program of the SDKPiL." Luxemburg's article was published in *Przegląd Robotniczy* [*The Workers' Magazine*] in 1904 and issued as a pamphlet in 1906.

3. The editorial board of the Menshevik *Iskra* [*The Spark*] moved to Vienna in 1905.

4. Dawid B. Goldendach-Riasanov (1870-1938), Russian social democrat, who joined the Mensheviks and in 1917 the Bolsheviks; a scholar, historian, and editor of Marxist classics; from 1921-1931, director of the Marx-Engels-Lenin Institute in Moscow. He was expelled from the party in 1931 and arrested.

5. Leon Trotsky (Lev D. Bronstein, 1879-1940), Russian revolutionary. While in czarist prison, he developed the theory of permanent revolution. He was one of the principal leaders in the founding of the USSR; people's commissar for foreign affairs under Lenin, from 1918 commissar of war and organizer of the Red Army. Advocating world revolution, he came into conflict with Stalin and in 1929 was banished from the USSR. In exile he founded the Fourth International. He was assassinated in Mexico in 1940. Author of *Literature and Revolution, Lenin, History of the Russian Revolution, The Revolution Betrayed, Stalin,* among other works.

6. Most probably a representative of the *Bund*.

7. *Z Pola Walki* [*From the Battlefield*], organ of the SDKPiL from January-October 1905, printed in Kraków and smuggled into Russian-annexed Poland. J. was its editor in chief. The story of the magazine telescopes the turbulent history of the Polish revolutionary movemont. First put out in Geneva, in 1889, *From the Battlefield* was devoted to the Great Proletariat party. Followed by the 1905 SDKPiL publication, it was revived in 1926 in Moscow by a group of Polish communists, to be closed in 1934 on the eve of Stalin's purges. In 1956, in the wake of the "Polish October," two issues were brought out in Warsaw. Started anew in 1958, it is currently published by the Institute for Workers' Movement of the Academy of Social Science at the Central Committee of the Polish United Workers' Party.

Letter 66

[Berlin]

[October 20, 1905]

Dear! This is in a hurry because I just got your letter with comments on "What [do we want?"] and at once got down to work to send it back by return mail, and let you breathe freely. I included *all* your comments except for two:

1. I can't figure out whether such details as the bicameral system, the responsibility of ministers, and so on belong in here, and if so, where. Let's keep it for the pamphlet anyhow, and by then we'll decide.

2. Concerning the Duma, you're absolutely wrong in insisting we must mention it here. Something's wrong with your head, my treasure. These are *comments on the program of permanent and general* importance, a statement of our *constructive* demands, not some article or campaign pamphlet meant to last but a few weeks or months. Everything about the Duma must be said in Marchlewski's pamphlet, and I'm not going to mention it here. I'll work on your further remarks as soon as I get them.

Yesterday by a strange coincidence I took out a box with mother's and father's last letters and old letters from Andzia and Józio. I read them through and cried until my eyes were swollen, and I went to bed wishing I'd never wake up. I cursed the damn "politics" that stopped me from answering father's and mother's letters for weeks on end. I never had time for them because of those world-shaking problems (and still nothing has changed). And my hate turned against you because you chained me to the accursed politics. I remembered that you persuaded me not to let Mrs. Lübeck come to Weggis lest she disturb my finishing the epoch-making article for [*Sozialistische*] *Monatshefte,* and she, she was coming with the news about my mother's death! See how honest I am with you.

Today I took a walk in the sun and I feel slightly better. Yesterday I was almost ready to give up, once and for all, the goddamn politics (or rather the bloody parody of our "political" life) and let the whole world go to hell. Politics is inane Baal worship, driving people—victims of their own obsession, of mental rabies—to sacrifice their entire existence. If I believed in God, I would be convinced that He would punish us gravely for this self-inflicted torment.

Hugs.

R.

Apropos, a small drama: Feldman from "Potemkin," nineteen years old (now he really is safely abroad), had an eighteen-year-old fiancée. In Geneva she heard the false rumor about his arrest and jumped out of a window to her death.

Letter 67

[Berlin]

Thursday

[October 26–27, 1905]

My dear Dyodyu! The Kautskys came by with the latest news about the fight in *Vorwärts* (the editorial), and we discussed the situation until it was too late for the mail. Enclosed is an article from [*Berliner*] *Tagebl*[*att*]. It is clear now I shall not escape the pleasure of writing for *Vorwärts* starting November 1st; we must consider it seriously.

Your brief, penciled note arrived today. I'd have gladly reconciled myself to the shortness of the letter because I know how much work you have. But even these few words sounded depressed and that touched me to the quick. Or is it just my imagination? Anyhow, it seems you can tell me now definitely what day you're coming since, because of the railroad strike, the Conference will probably come to nothing! And [*The Workers'*] *Magazine* is finished as you yourself wrote. [. . .]

Today I felt more keenly than ever the abnormality of my work in Polish affairs. I get an order from you: "Write an editorial about [Poland's] autonomy" (or about the Constituent Assembly)! Fine. But, damn it, in order to write it, I must read the Polish and the Russian press, I must be au courant with society's mood, I must be *in touch* with party affairs. Otherwise, all I can write are washed-out slogans, and I can't "hit the mark." The time when propaganda was made by expounding the party's constructive views is over. Now, every single question becomes part and parcel of the *party* struggle. And the old practice of limiting this struggle to the fight against the PPS is an outrageous anachronism. [. . .]

Friday. I had to stop last night because the Kautskys dropped by again to take me to Bebel's. Bebel wrote Kautsky that I should write the editorial for Tuesday (the first issue under the new leadership)[1], and Kautsky, the one for Wednesday. [. . .] There really was no need to see Bebel, as it turned out, but I didn't want to refuse Kautsky, and in general this has its uses. We sat and chatted, or rather listened, because as usual Bebel talked "all by himself" till eleven o'clock. It appears that the *entire* bourgeois press has sunk its teeth into the roast; the *Vossische* [*Zeitung*] devoted its editorial to it! Everywhere the "rrrevolutionary Rosa" is depicted as a holy terror. Bebel is as firm as iron.

As for your advice about rights and fees, pardon me, but this time, too, I'll do it my own way, following my instinct and my nature. Not in order to show my noble generosity, by no means, no! Still, I won't start out by haggling and making demands. Right now the crucial thing is to get rid of the others, to "clean the house of garbage"; what is developing is provisional by its very nature. This is the time to show what one *can do*—to appear petty and calculating would be very inappropriate. Anyhow, I don't feel in the least worried about rights and fees because when it comes to the Executive Committee (and also to the editors of *Vorwärts*—do you remember the fees for my Marx articles?), god knows I've no reason to complain. In short, everything will fall into place. Main thing: cold blood, a strictly correct attitude and solid performance from the start. Don't misunderstand me; in speaking about "provisional" I'm not thinking in terms of *months* but at the worst of a few weeks. [. . .]

I'm in a hurry to make the morning mail; so, many hugs for now, and I'll probably write again today if no one disturbs me!

Yours R.

1. By the order of the SPD Berlin Press Commission, six editors, revisionists, were fired from *Vorwärts* and replaced by a left-wing team, including Luxemburg. Besides her political differences with the former editorial board, L. had been critical of the German party journalism, which she considered "conventional," "wooden," "stereotyped." Letter to R. Seidel, June 23, 1898, in *Z Pola Walki*, 1959, No. 1(5), p. 69.

Letter 68

[Berlin]
[November 3, 1905]

My Dear! I received all your telegrams and just this minute your special delivery (double) letter came.

You ask why I haven't written, and how things are with me. Well, "What can I tell you, Herr Cohn?" I feel rotten.

Vorwärts, as you rightly noted, is rapidly descending to the level of *Sächsische Arbeiterzeitung,* and, what's worse, I'm the only one who understands it, as to some extent does K[autsky].

The editorial board is made up of morons, conceited morons to boot. "Journalist?"—not a single one. And besides,

Eisner & Co., along with a band of revisionists, are waging a ferocious press campaign against us, answered by either Bebel (!) or Cunow, or such-like (!!). I can only cover Russia, write an editorial now and then, offer good advice and suggestions, which, once carried out turn into such disaster that I want to tear my hair. A little example: right after "our" first issue (of November 1st), I told Strobel that his piece against Calver [revisionist] was worse than if Eisner himself had written it, that we didn't come to *Vorwärts* to shirk like cowards, that articles must be sharp and clear. The next day he said to me, "Well, now I shall do better, and you'll be pleased with me." And here, in today's issue, this dreadful blah-blah called "The Revolutionary Tempest," a mishmash of senseless clichés, "radical" gibberish, and this, no more no less, is the leading article in the "Political Review" section. Can one help screaming?

If you could just see their style! I want to jump out of my skin! Needless to say, all that is in store for us (that is, radicals) is utter disgrace.

And I see no way out because we have no *people*. Add to this that I'm *dog tired* and can barely drag my feet, and you'll have a complete picture. I go to the editorial office every day at 4 P.M., gabble with this gang until 9 P.M., and it drains the life out of me. Besides, I get up every day at 8 A.M. on the dot (since I've had the maid). Anguish keeps me awake at night, and I'm forever sleepy. In short, it is splendid.

I'm terribly happy about the work our people in Poland are doing. Unfortunately, I can put very little about it in *Vorwärts,* space is so scarce. I praised not the *Russian* Social Democracy but social democracy in the whole country, that is, *our* tactic in regard to the Duma, if you'll just read it carefully.

Hugs.
R.

Note: The following excerpts were prepared by the Russian police from letters found on Jogiches (alias Otto Engelmann) when he and Luxemburg (alias Anna Matschke) were arrested together in Warsaw in a pension owned by Countess Walewska. Annotated by the police, the fragments (some of which are presented here) survived and were translated back into Polish.

Letter 69

[Berlin–Friedenau]
[November 25, 1905]
Otto Engelman
Warsaw
Plac Zielony, Hotel Victoria

Police annotation: Letter in Polish with an envelope from Friedenau, postmark and address as above, contains, among others, the following excerpts:

It's driving me to despair that you're feeling wretched. Will it never end? Never? When will you stop thinking about what is aimless, senseless, and start living with what *is*? It hurt me that you feel so wretched because I remember what you once told me about those "poor boys who expect direction, help, and *moral* support from us." Do you remember? . . .

Yesterday Warski wired from Kraków asking you to go there. There's a letter from Op. in Warsaw, which I'll keep for you. Warski sent a special delivery letter asking for my opinion on some important questions regarding the organization of professional unions. . . .

I returned the passport to Ort. Munio [L.'s brother] will be here on Monday and we'll talk on the telephone. . . . Józio's [L.'s brother] children's nanny told me a lot about my family back home.

Yesterday I saw Kautsky and his wife. They told me outrageous stories that are being circulated about Par[vus]. He is pictured as a loafer, a fraud. Gorki is working at it systematically through his agents.[1] Tomorrow we're having a little conference (*some* conference!) at Kautsky's. G[orki's] agent is going to present "the proofs of P[arvus's] fraud."

1. Authorized by Maxim Gorki, Parvus collected royalties on Gorki's famous drama "The Lower Depths," staged in Germany, which he was to divide between the Social Democrats and the author, retaining a commission. Allegedly he embezzled the monies.

Letter 70

[Berlin–Friedenau]
[November 27, 1905]

Police annotation: Letter in Polish with the envelope addressed to Hotel Victoria, postmark as above, contains, among others, the following excerpts:

I'd been terribly worried about you (your safety and your health) when a postcard from Munio came saying he'd met with you in a café at 3:30. This morning I got a bunch of letters. Some of them (from Wurm, Mehring, Henrietta Holst)[1] express admiration for *Vorwärts*. I got one from Cezaryna [Wojnarowska] telling some tales (or perhaps the truth?) about Mendelson.[2] She says he's founded a national progressive party in Paris that is opposed to the PPS, that he has a report ready, and that he's on his way to Warsaw.

1. Henrietta Roland-Holst, active in the Dutch working movement, was a good acquaintance of L. She published a biography of L. in 1935.
2. Stanisław Mendelson (1858–1913), one of the first Polish Marxists; since 1884 in exile in Switzerland, France, and England. A founding member of the Polish Socialist Party (PPS), he ultimately broke with it.

Letter 71

[Berlin–Friedenau]
[November 28, 1905]

Police annotation: Letter in Polish, starting with the words "My golden Dyodyu," in which the author writes about her participation in a conference at Vorwärts, and says among other things:

I will send my statement for the congress by special delivery to your hotel or perhaps to Hanecki's because you may not go to your hotel often[1]. . . . Dyodyushek, be brave, calm, and cheerful. . . .

1. Jakub Fürstenberg-Hanecki, member of the Central Committee of the SDKPiL, veteran of the October Revolution. He was tried and executed in 1937 in the USSR and rehabilitated after 1956.

Unto Death . . .
1907–1914

During Luxemburg's absence, between December 1905 and September 1906, the SPD leaders had turned her empty apartment over to Konstantin [Costia] Zetkin, the twenty-two-year-old son of Luxemburg's close friend, Clara Zetkin. He remained there after her return, and they evidently became lovers, as Jogiches learned when he arrived in Berlin the following spring. "If comrade R[osa] L[uxemburg's] friend stays in Berlin for good and lives in her apartment, then Costia can hardly remain there," commented August Bebel to Karl Kautsky on April 15, 1907.[1] Jogiches did stay in Berlin, though not in Luxemburg's house.

Luxemburg's love affair with Zetkin never attained the depth of intimacy and intellectual affinity that tied her to Jogiches. But with Zetkin she was worshipped, adored, admired, as she had long yearned to be. Years before she had written Jogiches: ". . . I constantly see *the kind of women* men live with, how those men worship them and yield to their domination, and all the time, in the back of my mind, I am aware of the way you treat me. . . ." (letter 35). For the next few years Zetkin became the recipient of Luxemburg's letters, which were in a sense more intimate than those she was currently writing to Jogiches.

As the member of the Central Committee of the SDKPiL, Jogiches was still Luxemburg's party leader whose authority, but not necessarily judgment, she never questioned. Neither Zetkin nor anyone else could ever take over the role he played in her life as an intellectual and political alter ego. Though Jogiches moved to a small hotel in Steglitz, shortly after his return to Berlin, he refused to give back the keys to her apartment, as he refused, in vain, to give her up. Dramatic scenes followed, with Jogiches threatening to kill her and her lover, and Luxemburg acquiring a revolver for self-defense.

Nevertheless, in 1908, a year after the breach, as Luxemburg wrote to Konstantin Zetkin, Jogiches was working in her apartment during the day and leaving at night. The library they had assembled over the years remained in her flat, an excuse for Jogiches to be a frequent, if unwelcome, guest (letter 75).

After a two-year lapse in their correspondence, her letters to Jogiches, bearing neither salutation nor signature, were sent from the home they had once shared to his hotel room. For two years she used an impersonal form, elaborately avoiding any kind of personal pronoun. For example, referring to Jogiches's brother, she wrote "the brother," to avoid the pronoun "your"; she replaced "you" with Jogiches's residence and wrote, ". . . Steglitz should make sure. . . ." Some time later she switched to the second person plural, and five years after their intimacy had ceased she occasionally addressed Jogiches, "Moi Drodzy," in that context roughly meaning "Dear Comrade." Finally, in 1913 she began to sign her letters "R."

Political duties sometimes brought them together, as in May 1907 at the Fifth Congress of the Russian Social-Democratic Workers' Party in London, but she stringently avoided personal contact. She kept looking for another apartment to put an end to his unexpected visits and in 1911 moved from

Friedenau to Südende. Three years passed before he obtained her permission to come to her place to discuss party affairs.

By 1909, in addition to notes and memos, she wrote letters in which her dependence on him, her need of him, and the closeness they once shared breaks through; she complained of frequent headaches, nervous exhaustion, depression. Nor did she try to conceal her loneliness. But these were statements of fact, not attempts to woo him. As in the old days, she was anxious to have Jogiches comment on her work, and, as always, he spared her neither his criticism nor his reprimands.

Money, too, remained an issue. Now it was not Jogiches she asked for loans but "the party" (letter 91)—purely a matter of semantics. Since October 1907 when she accepted the chair in political economy at the SPD Central Party School, her income, supplemented by her journalism, was by no means modest. But she never learned the art of counting money. Nor did she care to.

In 1907 she spent two months in prison for "inciting to violence," that is, for appealing to the Germans to follow the example of the revolutionary Russian proletariat. She devoted the years 1908–1914 to working on "The National Question and Autonomy," a vision of today's world torn by ethnic and national strife; on *The Accumulation of Capital*; and on the *Introduction to Political Economy* (published posthumously in 1925). She made dozens of speeches at meetings, rallies, congresses, and published close to two hundred articles and pamphlets denouncing militarism as inevitably leading to war and as an immediate danger.

In February 1914 she stood trial for inciting to public disobedience. "Should they believe that we are going to lift the murderous weapons against our French and other brethren, we shall cry out loudly, *'we will not do it!'*" Speaking in her own defense at the criminal court in Frankfurt am Main, she charged her accusers of violating people's rights by dragging them into a war that was not theirs. Her speech, a masterpiece of oratory, turned the courtroom into a socialist platform. In closing, she addressed the prosecutor, who had asked for her immediate arrest lest she flee. "Sir," she said, "I believe *you* would run away. A Social Democrat never does. A Social Democrat stands by his deeds and laughs at your judgments."

Although some Germans failed to understand why so much tolerance should be accorded to "the impertinent behavior of this woman," who on top of insulting the German army was a "rootless" outsider with no *Vaterland* of her own, Luxemburg's speeches against war echoed throughout Germany. They were also heard at the congresses of the helpless Socialist International.

In June 1914, she again stood trial, this time in Berlin after the Prussian Minister of War, General von Falkenhayn, had her indicted for accusing the army of maltreating soldiers. The trial turned into one of her greatest triumphs. Over one thousand soldiers came forth to testify for the defense. And it was about this trial that she wrote her last known words to Jogiches: "Tomorrow, as soon as everything is over, I will phone you the verdict. But—it might get late."

1. *August Bebels Briefwechsel mit Karl Kautsky*, Karl Kautsky, Jr., ed. (Assen: Van Gorcum & Co., N.V., 1971), p. 184.

Police identification, Warsaw, 1906

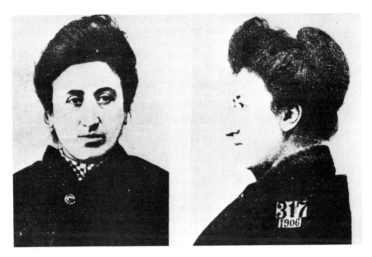

Prison cell in Wronki, 1916-1917

In 1907

Leo Jogiches, probably 1908

With Konstantin Zetkin in Berlin, around 1910

Berlin, 1910

Letter 72

[Berlin]
[June 6 or 7, 1908]

If it is absolutely necessary to consult about the article, etc.,
it must be *tomorrow,* since Tuesday or Wednesday I must go
to the seashore with my sister. I will send the article about autonomy for the next issue of *The Social-Democratic Review*
from there.[1] I cannot promise to write the editorial. If there is
no alternative, my autonomy article may be used as an
editorial.

I wrote to Led[ebour].

1. *The Social-Democratic Review* [*Przegląd Socjaldemokratyczny*], a theoretical organ of the SDKPiL.

Letter 73

[Berlin]
[ca. June 12, 1908?]

It was impossible to get the deposit from the bank as I did
not have the faintest idea of the balance. I must have the bank
book or the exact figure beside their last statement on which
the signature [Jogiches's] is required. Could not add anything
to the article. It was as trashy as before, and I tore it up.

Letter 74

[Berlin]
[April 1909?]

Radek sent the review.[1] I will return it tomorrow (Sunday)
morning. I am simply unable to write the proclamation for the
recruits. I *cannot* write popular trash—I wasted two days
trying. It's not that I do not want to, I absolutely cannot.

1. Karol Sobelson, pseudonym Radek (1885-1939), a Polish revolutionary, member of the SDKPiL and, in Russia, of the All-Union Communist Party. He was a brilliant journalist, one of the most colorful revolutionary figures. He perished in the purge of Polish communists in the USSR.

Letter 75

[Berlin]
[September, 1909?]

Yesterday's conversation left me so unnerved that I stayed awake half the night; even today I am completely unable to work.

As countless times before, I must again ask [you] to discuss business with me in writing and to leave me in peace in my own home.[1] I do not need the other room; I never set foot in it.[2] Whoever stays with me is put up in my room in order to keep out of that room. But in my apartment I must feel at home, not as if I were in a hotel where anyone can come and go whether I like it or not.

I cannot bear this wrangling any longer—I've asked [you] so many times to stop it. All summer long I kept moving from place to place just to stay away from the house, and now it is the same thing all over again. Throughout the summer the letters [to Jogiches] were delivered without me acting as a go-between, now everything is coming to my address again, and the newspapers, too, must be picked up [by Jogiches] every week.

I cannot go on like this. I do what I can for *The* [*Social-Democratic*] *Review* and for *The* [*Red*] *Banner*. I am ready, if necessary, to substitute as editor, but I want a home of my own. If there is no way I can have it, I prefer to give up the whole apartment together with the maid and to sublet a furnished room just so I would know that I am living at home, not in a hotel. I request a reply as to whether this is going to continue because I must know what to do with myself.

1. Jogiches, as a member of the Central Committee of the SDKPiL, was L.'s superior. She continued to be active in Polish affairs and to write for the party publications.
2. In possession of the keys to the flat they once had shared, Jogiches kept using "the other room" as his study during the day, leaving only at night. He kept his books and clothes in his former room and also came to pick up the mail and papers addressed to his former residence.

Letter 76

[Berlin]

[ca. November 15, 1909]

The brother's [Jogiches's brother Pavel] letter, which I en-close, arrived with a check for 107 Marks drawn to the Deutsche Bank.[1] The bank only cashed it today. I am forward-ing 100 Fr and I shall keep 25 M and 40 pf until [your] return.

As yet no manuscripts have arrived. Mehring refused. I asked K[autsky] to give us the article scheduled for publication in *Vorwärts* on the 22nd. He promised to write it one of these days, depending on his health (he has been slightly in-disposed).

The [*Social-Democratic*] *Review* arrived a few days ago.

Munio [Maksymilian Luxemburg] confirmed with the brother the receipt of the check and urged him to send more.

In view of the form of the remittance, I request a confirma-tion of the receipt of 100 Fr by return mail.

Note: Jogiches refused to accept the 100 Fr and answered as follows:[2]

I very much regret being so insistent, but I am inclined to believe that there's something wrong here, that perhaps Munio was unable to return the money[3] and you[4] are returning it in his stead. This I absolutely do not want because I consider

Munio an acquaintance of *mine* and, as any other acquaintance, he may be unable to return the money, which ought not in the least involve his relatives. Since I am not certain, I prefer not to touch the money and am returning it, enclosed.

1. Paweł Jogiches, in charge of the family business in Wilno, had been transferring Leo Jogiches's share to him, often using Maksymilian (Munio) Luxemburg as a go-between in order to cover J.'s traces. Munio transferred the money to his sister. Hence L.'s involvement in J.'s financial affairs.
2. This note of Jogiches's and the next one survived only because Luxemburg wrote on the back of his notes. Jogiches meticulously saved Luxemburg's every written word for posterity.
3. Jogiches refers to money he loaned to Maksymilian Luxemburg.
4. Until their intimacy ceased, L. and J. addressed one another as "thou." The usage of the English pronoun "you" blunts, in translation, the dramatic difference in tone after they had broken up. Here J. uses the second person plural (the equivalent of the French *vous* or the German *sie*), as does L. whenever she uses the personal pronoun.

Note: On the back of Jogiches's letter L. answered:

Letter 77

[Berlin]
[ca. November 20, 1909]

I don't understand what is going on. If you don't want your money, send it back to Munio. I wrote him that I had received and forwarded it, and the rest is no concern of mine.

Let me point out (in case of [your] writing to Munio) that I took the liberty of telling him once that you need money, so he has obviously sent it now.

Note: Jogiches answered,

In that case let me have the receipt please.

Note: On the back of Jogiches's answer L. replied,

I cannot search the trash barrel for the receipt. Kindly get in touch with Munio and do not bother me.

Letter 78

[Berlin]
[end of April 1910]

Trotsky called on me today. He talked at length about Russian affairs and complained that Warski is supporting the Bolsheviks. He sends his regards and a message from Innokentii[1] that he is going to see Józef.[2] Anyway, Innokentii settled it directly which, to be on the safe side, I told Trotsky.

1. Josif F. Dubrowiński, pseudonym Innokentii, Russian revolutionary.
2. Feliks Dzierżyński, pseudonym Józef (1877-1926), Polish revolutionary, member of the Central Committee of the SDKPiL, one of the organizers of the October Revolution, Lenin's closest supporter among the Poles, head of the Cheka (The Extraordinary Commission to Combat Counterrevolution and Sabotage). According to Radek, L. was saddened that Dzierżyński accepted the post. "Terror has never defeated us," she said in 1918 upon hearing the news. "Why should we have to depend on it now." Quoted in *Rosa Luxemburg* by J. P. Nettl (London: Oxford University Press, 1966), vol. II, p. 731.

Letter 79

[Berlin]
[April 29, 1910]

A certain "Basia" from Poland was here today.[1] I sent her to the soup [unidentified code name]. If it is possible [for you] to get in touch with her, a message should be left at the soup telling her when and where she should report. She strikes me as somewhat insane. Should letters come tomorrow and Sunday, Ida [the maid] will forward them at once. I will be home Monday.

1. Barbara Szpiro, member of the SDKPiL, later of the Polish Communist Party, and subsequently of the All-Union Communist Party (b) in the Soviet Union.

Letter 80

[Berlin]
[ca. July 18, 1910]

I am returning Win's poem, which I found very beautiful. There is no reason to wait until the whole page is set. I do not think a newspaper should be symmetrical, trimmed like an English lawn. Rather, it should be somewhat untamed, like a wild orchard, so that it will pulsate with life and shine with young talents. [. . .]

Letter 81

[Aeschi, Switzerland]
[August 1 or 2, 1910]

A request: Have Krakus send me a few new Polish novels *immediately*.[1] I don't have a *single* work of fiction. The books he reviewed for the *Tribune,* etc.

Note: On August 3, 1910, Jogiches wrote from Berlin to F. Dierżyński in Kraków, "Would you take two or three works of fiction (I'll tell you which) out of Gumplowicz's library and send them to Rosa in Switzerland. I'll be happy to cover the expense, of course."

1. Henryk Stein, pseudonym Krakus, member of the SDKPiL, the Polish Communist Party, and later of the All-Union Communist Party (b) in the Soviet Union. He was also a journalist and literary critic.

Letter 82

[Aeschi, Switzerland]
[August 5, 1910]

I am in a fine mess. *Vorwärts* refused to publish my article, a very important one, about the Baden [social democrats]. *Neue Zeit* refused to publish my reply (murderous) to Mehring (No. 44 NZ). I've sent the first to *Dortmunder [Arbeiter-zeitung]*, the second to *Leipziger [Volkszeitung]*. Don't know whether they'll accept. (In Dortmund, Haenisch is away on vacation, the others are cowards, and Lensch is, on the whole, unreliable.) Just now I received No. 45 [of *Neue Zeit*] with Kautsky's "answer."[1] He wriggles like a cornered snake. I'll write again to at least set straight the charge about the "distorted quotation." But Kautsky will probably again refuse to take it. With me far away he feels secure. Besides, he has nothing to lose. The material for *The Society* hasn't arrived yet, why?

1. Twelve years of friendship and close collaboration between L. and Kautsky ended when L. accused him, and gradually the entire SPD leadership, of theorizing about the revolution rather than working toward it. In her article "Die Theorie und die Praxis" ["Theory and Practice"] L., quoting Engels, charged Kautsky with distorting Marx's and Engels's theories. Kautsky, in turn, charged L. with "distorting quotations" from Engels. The polemic continued with L.'s article "Zur Richtigstellung" ["Correction"] published in *Neue Zeit* on August 19, 1910.

Letter 83

[Magdeburg or Berlin]
Friday night
[September 23, 1910]

Letter received. I feel like a beaten dog, and it seems I've suffered a shattering defeat.[1] Can't describe everything.

Please read the report in V[*orwärts*] and come on Saturday, that is tomorrow, to Friedenau [to her apartment], but not later than 5 P.M. because I want to go to bed early. Let me explain this much: the coauthors of the motion, afraid they would end up in the minority, forced me to withdraw it! . . .[2] I'd like to know what impression the whole story has made. The rest I'll tell personally. However, I must say this in advance: I am physically *finished*. To get to work for the next two to three days is out of the question. I cannot think, sleep, or eat. It's a mystery to me how I'll prepare for the important lecture at the metal workers' meeting on the first.

All my health and energy for the next two months to come has been used up by the party congress.

I'll be waiting, then, at 5 P.M. (no later, please, it will be late anyhow when I get to bed.)

1. L. refers to the debate at the SPD party congress in Magdeburg where the issue of universal suffrage was discussed.
2. L. presented a motion, opposed by the right wing of the SPD, to use mass strike as a weapon in the struggle for universal suffrage. In effect the motion was withdrawn before voting.

Letter 84

[Berlin]
[ca. October 9, 1910]

It's awful—I suffered the whole day from such acute physical and moral depression that I was unable *to write a single sentence*.[1] I've been sitting for the entire day until now (8 P.M.) over the introduction to the reprint of the Polish Question and couldn't squeeze anything out. I feel like throwing up and must go to bed. [. . .]

1. Responding to J.'s immediate question, L. explained the next day, "Concerning my depression, nothing has happened; it is a depression pure and simple and therefore still more annoying. . . ."

Letter 85

[Berlin]
[October 11, 1910]

It is essential to include news about the general strike of French railway workers that has just broken out (*chemin de fer du Nord* is all on strike). Today's late edition of [*Berliner*] *Tageblatt*!

N.B. I just noticed the quotation in the *Tribune* article (last paragraph, red pencil) on the Jewish question. It may be crucial to my article about *Pravda*. If so, insert it yourself. *Tribune* enclosed.

Letter 86

[Berlin]
February 23 [1911]

Enclosed is the paper [the passport] for Warski. It cost 15 M, which I advanced and want returned.

Yesterday I immediately wrote to [Clara] Z[etkin] to send me Lenin's letter, asking her not to answer it before getting in touch with me. Wouldn't it be best if she wrote Lenin, without mincing words, that she'd get in touch with *me* and do what I consider necessary? Or, if need be, she can write him saying she'll get in touch with *you*.[1] This should do for L[enin].

More about the rest later.

Apropos, Wiethölter [Jogiches's tailor] is on my back.[2]

1. At the Fifth Congress of the Russian Social-Democratic Workers' Party in London, in May 1907, J. had been elected a deputy member of the Central Committee of the party.
2. Probably J. owed his tailor money. Earlier, L. informed J., "The tailor delivered the suit." And on August 10, 1910, she wrote, ". . . if W[iethölter] was indeed paid in May, three months in advance, he obviously got wind of the chaos in our accounts and *knowingly takes advantage* of it."

Letter 87

[Berlin]
[March 1911?]

I must finally ask [you] to confirm the receipt of the money—this much is owed to *me*. One should understand that since the money comes to *my* address, [your] stubborn silence puts me in the position of a thief who has pocketed the money. Is this clear at last? It is beyond me how one can have so little consideration for others in as sensitive a matter as honesty in financial affairs.[1]

The feuilleton, again, made me want to throw up.

1. As in letters 76 and 77, L. refers to money sent for J. via her brother, Maksymilian.

Letter 88

[Berlin]
[March 31, 1912]

Today total victory in the General Assembly [of the SPD delegates for Greater Berlin]. Despite the defense by the executive committee of the three (Haase, Braun, and Molkenbuhr), the resolution against them was accepted by all except perhaps 12 of the 900 delegates![1] My mandate was not questioned.

I'm about to start the May article for [*The Red*] *Banner*.

But! *What about the loan for me!* This is very urgent! Please get it settled in writing if Dzierżyński isn't coming. Otherwise, I'll be left penniless after the first.

(N.B. My articles were the only ones reprinted and the Kautskyites are furious.)

1. L. presented a motion concerning a runoff election to the Reichstag.

Letter 89

[Berlin]
[beginning of April 1912]

Your lengthy reprimand was totally inappropriate. After you had left, I got a migraine and was unable to do anything, and next morning I had no one to send to the post office. Nothing is lost though—[*Vorwärts*] ruined my note anyway. [. . .]

Letter 90

[Berlin]
[July 1912]

I was sick (partly after reading the dissenters' publications)[1] and wrote the article first thing on Wednesday. Since you wrote that you'd be back at the *latest* on Thursday, I haven't sent it to Kraków.

The article is too long, but I didn't want to cut it before you read it. Am expecting you tomorrow (Sunday) *before dinner*.

N.B. I'd like to sign the article "R. L." if the Central Committee [of the SDKPiL of which J. was a member] agrees.

1. In 1911, the SDKPiL split into supporters of the Central Committee in Berlin and dissenters, with a National Committee created in 1914 in Kraków.

Letter 91

[Berlin]
[August 1912]

I'm enclosing more galleys, which are now coming in promptly.[1] I must start returning them. Kindly send further news on Radek and other affairs. I feel very poorly, but not on account of the news—just in general. Now, business: can the party lend me 150–200 M by the first? I'll return it in a month together with the whole debt. Kindly answer. Got a mandate from Oberrhein and, unfortunately, will have to go to Chemnitz.

1. J. was proofreading L.'s *The Accumulation of the Capital,* as in 1898 he had proofread her first work, *The Industrial Development of Poland.*

Letter 92

[Berlin]
[beginning of October 1912]

Enclosed is Lenin's "bombshell."[1] Why don't you send me an outline of the answer. If possible promptly, and, if possible, *concise.*

1. Lenin's pamphlet "Zur gegenwärtigen Sachlage in der sozial-demokratischen Arbeiterpartei Russlands" was published in German in September 1912. It discussed, as the title indicates, the current situation in the Russian Social-Democratic Workers' Party.

Letter 93

[Berlin]
[May 28, 1913]

Yesterday I had an excellent meeting in Leipzig in the biggest hall there. I spoke about world politics and sharply criticized the fraction and the adopted tactic.[1] I got thundering applause and public thanks. After the meeting a fellow from our section, a very nice boy, came up to me, and so did three Bolsheviks. They pressured me to talk at their meeting; I barely got out of it. Our young fellow knew Warski is in Poland! From Warski himself!

Enclosed is the envelope, which looks a little suspicious to me.

1. In 1906 the PPS [Polish Socialist Party] split, with Józef Pilsud-
ski forming the PPS Revolutionary Fraction.

Postcard 94

[London]
Sunday
[December 14, 1913]

I'm going back tomorrow morning (my migraine permitting).
It seems we suffered a complete defeat at the meeting, though
through no fault of mine.[1] Plekhanov didn't come,[2] neither did
Lenin. The Bolsheviks were represented by a complete idiot,[3]
while the Mensheviks came in droves. Kautsky (on behalf of
the German executive committee) introduced a resolution right
away recommending that the executive of the Bureau reach an
agreement "with all who consider themselves social democrats!" I opposed the resolution, but I was entirely isolated;
the scoundrel just kept messing things up. The rest personally.

1. Meeting of the International Bureau of the Socialist International. Kautsky's motion (accepted) called for a meeting of all the
different Russian social democratic factions. Luxemburg's motion
(withdrawn) called for a "unification congress" aimed toward
unifying the Russian Social-Democratic Workers' Party, split in
1903 into Bolsheviks and Mensheviks.
2. Georgii V. Plekhanov (1857-1918), Russian revolutionary and
philosopher, is considered to be the founder of Russian Marxism.
Opposed to political terror, he broke with the Populists, left Russia in 1880, and spent most of his exile in Switzerland. He collaborated with Lenin in publishing *Iskra* [*The Spark*] but generally opposed Bolshevism. In 1917 he returned to Russia, but fled to
Finland in 1918 after openly denouncing the Bolshevik Revolution
as a coup d'état.
3. M. M. Litvinov (1876-1951), an early Bolshevik. After the
Munich pact he was replaced by Molotov as foreign commissar.
He was ambassador to the United States from 1941 to 1943.

Letter 95

[Berlin]
[1913?]

After yesterday's "conference" I couldn't sleep all night and am unable to work today. Therefore, the note will be written only tomorrow. I request that I be notified with a word or two if a consultation is necessary lest you rush in here in the midst of my work and, without any benefit to the party, turn my day's and evening's schedule upside down.

Letter 96

[Berlin]
[1913?]

It is almost midnight. I am working on the article. I feel very sick (I had trouble with my stomach during the night) and that's why it was so hard to get started. But now I am writing, and it seems this will be a splendid article.

Tomorrow morning, as usual on Wednesdays, I don't teach, so I will finish and send it off at noon.[1] The article will most certainly be finished tomorrow, so I am asking for extra time because I must lie down; my eyes just won't stay open.

1. L. was professor of economics at the SPD Central Party School in Berlin. One of her students was Wilhelm Pieck, president of the German Democratic Republic from 1949. Another was Mrs. Rosi Frölich, whose husband, Paul, wrote *Rosa Luxemburg, Gedanke und Tat* (Paris: Editions Nouvelles Internationales, 1939). In the summer of 1978 Mrs. Frölich kindly shared with me reminiscences about her teacher. Luxemburg differed from the typical European professor in that she did not conduct classes by just delivering lectures. Interested in each individual, she wanted her students to understand and to know; concerned with their views, she used her knowledge to broaden theirs.

Letter 97

[Berlin]

[1913]

It seems to me the article is poor. I feel very sick, and I forced myself to squeeze it out, and I cannot do any better. It can be changed at will. However, I request (1) "Jerusalem" should not be corrected but left in the feminine gender; (2) *proporzec* [pennon] is a fine Polish word: genitive—*proporca*.

If the ending seems too coarse, it can be replaced by: Hands off, ye mangy Cerberuses of Capital.

Kindly let me know if the article is any good.

I am going to bed.

Letter 98

[1913?]

I am missing two books which I urgently need. Will you please check and *write* me at once whether by any chance you have them:

1. Max Eyth, *Lebendige Kräfte (7 Vorträge der Technik)*.
2. A volume of Shakespeare in German translation, red-golden cover.

Should you have either, kindly bring it on Monday when you come.

Would you drop in tomorrow, on Sunday, at my sister-in-law's for a short while.[1] Holsteinischestr. No. 39. I think it's on the ground floor, a sublet, furnished room.

1. L. scrupulously reminded J. of her family's anniversaries. In 1910 she informed him, "on February seventh was Andzia's [L.'s sister] wedding anniversary." Some time later she wrote, "Edyush's [L.'s nephew] birthday was today, that is, on the fourteenth. S[abina] F[einstein] is leaving tomorrow. She could take a small present for him."

Letter 99

[1913?]

Your addition is an aberration of taste. The article doesn't need any *pointe*, kindly do not spoil it.

Letter 100

[1913?]

I must know the relationship the party has now with that philosopher [not identified] and whether it's worth my while to answer him fully. Return the letter at once, please.

Letter 101

[Berlin]
[beginning of April, 1914]

Of course, I must have had the check in my hand ten times while I was looking for it, and I still didn't see it. It is enclosed. Thanks for the materials; they arrived in time. My address will most probably be Chailly sur Clarens, *poste restante*.

As for the photo, having thought it over, I'll follow your advice: *without* a hat. I've already sent the Seidels your regards. I'll write them from Switzerland. On my way back I plan to stop in Munich in order to talk with Ernst [editor of *Süddeutscher Postillon*].

Mehring promised to talk to Wallfisch (who is now publishing his articles on militarism in pamphlet form). M[ehring] left *Bremer* [*Bürgerzeitung*]. N.B. Evchen [Eva Mehring] was the first to draw his attention to the impropriety, with regard to me, of dividing the publishing costs.[1] He was indignant, but I said of course that it didn't matter.

Instead of "asking" the maid when it is convenient for her, it is best just to come here between 3 and 5 P.M. I'll simply tell her she must stay at home and *basta*.

The Polish and Russian materials are on the big shelf in the
library over the sofa—to the right and to the left.
Schulz—Victoriastr. 5.

1. After they were expelled in 1913 from *Leipziger Volkszeitung*, because they represented the extreme left, Luxemburg, Mehring,
and Marchlewski founded a bulletin *Sozialdemokratische Korrespon-
denz*.

Letter 102

[Berlin]
[June 13, 1914]

Yesterday we decided *not* to request an adjournment[1] because Rosenfeld[2] had heard that the prosecutor was trying to
find out when my case comes before the *Reichsgericht*.[3] This
means they are eager to have the *Reichsgericht*'s verdict *before* the trial opens in order to mete out a stiffer sentence. That
is why *we want* the opposite. Your remark (concerning the
priority of the *Vorwärts* trial)[4] is very important and proves the
correctness of our decision. So, the trial opens on the 29th.
The time is short, and our preparation is for the birds. But we
have witnesses. Some are already coming forward. We have
145 and can count on some 200 before the trial starts. As the
trial proceeds more witnesses will speak up. [. . .]

1. L. was indicted for publicly accusing the army of maltreating
soldiers. The trial opened in Berlin on June 29, 1914. Soldiers, the
victims of abuse, 1013 of them, volunteered to testify for the defense. Afraid of adverse publicity, the authorities suspended the
trial over L.'s protests.
2. Dr. Kurt Rosenfeld, L.'s attorney.
3. In February 1914, L. stood trial for inciting public disobedience
and was sentenced to one year in prison. The appeal was pending
in the Reich Superior Court when she faced the War Ministry's
indictment. With the Frankfurt sentence enforced, the Berlin sentence was likely to be stiffer.

4. Three editors of *Vorwärts* tracked down and published a story about corruption in the Prussian army; two high-ranking officers had been bribed by horse dealers supplying the army.

Letter 103

[Berlin]

[July 2, 1914]

We have about seven hundred witnesses. Tomorrow, as soon as everything is over, I will phone you the verdict. But— it might get late.

As the year 1914 approached, Luxemburg's thoughts reflected the anxiety expressed previously by Heinrich Heine, "German thunder is of true German character; it is not very nimble, but rumbles along somewhat slowly. But come it will, and when ye hear a crashing such as has never been heard before in world's history, then know that the German thunderbolt has struck at last." German foreign politics led to a catastrophe, and on top of this the German social democrats were frustrating Luxemburg's efforts to avert the war. A united front of the international proletariat, her dream and her religion, died before it was born.

When the war broke out, Luxemburg contemplated suicide. Her world, public and private, had fallen to pieces. Socialists throughout Europe enthusiastically voted in war budgets; workers of different nationalities turned into implacable enemies overnight. "The spectacle is over," Luxemburg wrote a year later. ". . . The trains carrying the reservists are now leaving in silence without the ecstatic farewells of fair maidens. . . . The crisp atmosphere of the pale rising day is filled with the voices of a different chorus: the hoarse clamor of the hyenas and vultures reaping the battlefields. Ten thousand tents, regular size, high quality!! One hundred thousand kilograms of bacon, cocoa powder,

ersatz coffee, immediate delivery, cash only! Grenades,
lathes, ammunition pouches, matchmakers for war widows
. . . serious offers only! The hurray-patriotic, widely adver-
tised cannon fodder . . . is already rotting in the battlefields.
. . . Disgraced, shameful, bloodstained, filthy—that's the true
face of bourgeois society. . . . The well-groomed, cosmetic
mask of virtue, culture, philosophy, and ethics, order, peace,
and constitution slips, and its real, naked self is exposed.
The rapacious beast breaks loose, the infernal sabbath of
anarchy erupts, and the bourgeoisie's plague-infested breath
spells the doom of mankind and culture. . . . During this
witches' sabbath a disaster of world-wide magnitude occurred: the capitulation of the international social democracy."[1] This disaster precipitated the birth of Nazi Germany
and of Stalinism.

From February 1915 until November 1918, except for a brief
respite in 1916, Luxemburg was incarcerated "for her own
protection." If her passion was broken by captivity and
depression, her faith was not. In prison she wrote the famous
Junius Pamphlet, appealing to the sound instincts of the proletariat, warning that the ultimate choice was between "socialism and barbarism." Even though "millions of proletari-
ans of all nationalities were felled at the front line of shame,
of fratricide, of self-destruction, the song of slaves on their
lips," she believed, "we are not lost and would conquer had
we not forgotten how to learn." "Indeed, we are like Jews,"
she wrote, "whom Moses is leading through the desert."[2]

Jogiches, separated by prison bars, became close again. He
took care of her needs, and she responded. He was back in
her life. Politics, as ever, held them together, as did her faith
that perhaps not everything was lost. While she was in
prison, he, significantly, for the first time became involved
in German affairs. From 1916 he was the leader of the SPD
left opposition, *Spartakusbund,* editor of its organ, *Spartakus-
briefe,* cofounder of the German Communist Party, and even-

tually, after Luxemburg's death, secretary general of its Central Committee.

On November 10, 1918, the day after she was set free, Luxemburg was in Berlin. Until her death Jogiches was constantly at her side. The tempests and rancor behind them, their friendship, their spiritual affinity, passed all tests. Now they struggled together for the dream of their youth—the revolution. Resentment and hostility toward the Bolshevik government in Russia, and mob hysteria clutching beaten soldiers and hungry civilians in Germany, seemed to matter little. Convinced that "In Russia the problem could only be posed. In Russia it could not be solved," Luxemburg set out to solve it in Germany. On New Year's Eve, 1918, she delivered her last speech at the founding congress of the German Communist Party. "If the proletariat fails to fulfill its duty as a class," she said, "if the proletariat fails to make socialism a reality, we shall all go down to a common doom."[3]

She knew her days were numbered; she had neither the strength nor the will to live. On January 14 her last article appeared in *Die Rote Fahne* under the ironical title "Order Reigns in Berlin." An "order," she wrote, whose survival depends on ever-new bloodshed, on ever-new slaughter, "inexorably proceeds toward its historical fate—annihilation."

Rosa Luxemburg was murdered on January 15, 1919, her corpse thrown into a canal. Her assassins, the *Freikorps,* joined forces with Hitler's storm troops a short time later. Jogiches, his doom sealed in Berlin, refused to leave the city, determined to bring her murderers to justice. He was assassinated two months later.

1. Róża Luksemburg, *Wybór Pism* (Warsaw: Książka i Wiedza, 1959), vol. II, pp. 255-257.
2. Ibid., p. 268.
3. Ibid., p. 483.

Leo Jogiches during World War I

Landwehr Canal where Luxemburg's assassins threw her body on the night of January 15, 1919. It was washed up on May 31.

A symbolic funeral—Luxemburg's coffin is empty. Berlin, January 25, 1919.

The funeral. Under Luxemburg's picture the closing words of her last article published in *Die Rote Fahne*, January 14, 1919. "The revolution," she wrote, "will come back any day to announce: 'I was, I am, I shall be.'"

Appendix: Historical Note

From its inception the Polish socialist movement was split over the issue of regaining national sovereignty. As the result of three successive partitions—1772, 1793, 1795—Poland disappeared from the map of Europe, divided and annexed until 1918 by Russia, Prussia, and Austria. Lithuania (with its capital, Wilno), which merged with Poland at the end of the fourteenth century, also passed to Russia, as eventually did the central part of Poland (capital, Warsaw).

The first Polish workers' party *Proletariat,* founded by Ludwik Waryński in 1882 in the wake of two unsuccessful insurrections in 1830 and 1863, was based on the principle of proletarian internationalism. It denigrated the traditional national sentiment, urging the primacy of workers' rights and the improvement of their condition. National liberation was to come along with the collapse of capitalism and the victory of a socialist world revolution.

The Polish Socialist Party (PPS), founded in 1892, subordinated socialist goals to national independence. Józef Piłsudski, a leading member of the PPS and founder of its organ *Robotnik* [*The Worker*], organized and assumed command of the Polish army to fight for Poland's independence. It was proclaimed in 1918.

The Social Democracy of the Kingdom of Poland (SDKP), a spiritual heir of *Proletariat,* was founded in 1893 by Rosa Luxemburg, Leo Jogiches, Feliks Dzierżyński, Julian Marchlewski, and others and in 1900 reorganized as the Social Democracy of the Kingdom of Poland and Lithuania (SDKPiL). Its goal was the implementation of Marx's theories and, in the short run, a liberal constitution for the entire Russian empire with territorial autonomy for Poland. The different goals of these two parties, Marxist socialism and Polish independence, irreconcilably divided the SDKPiL and the PPS.

In 1918 the SDKPiL was succeeded by the Polish Communist Party (KPP). Decimated in Stalin's purges and dissolved as a "provocateur" party, it was revived in 1942 as the Polish Workers' Party (PPR) and merged in 1948 with the Polish Socialist Party (PPS), becoming the Polish United Workers' Party (PZPR), the ruling power in contemporary Poland.

List of Letters

The First Years: 1893–1897

1	Clarens, Switzerland, March 21, 1893
2	Paris, March 25, 1894
3	Paris, April 5, 1894
4	Paris, March 21, 1895
5	Paris, March 28, 1895
6	Switzerland, July 16, 1897

The Trial: 1898–1900

7	Berlin, May 17, 1898
8	Berlin, May 28, 1898
9	Berlin, May 31, 1898
10	Legnica, June 14, 1898
11	Legnica, June 15, 1898
12	Berlin, June 24, 1898
13	Berlin, June 27, 1898
14	Berlin, July 2, 1898
15	Berlin, July 10, 1898
16	Berlin, August 22, 1898
17	Berlin, September 2, 1898
18	Berlin, September 6, 1898
19	Berlin, September 10, 1898
20	Berlin, September 25, 1898

21   Berlin, December 3, 1898
22   Berlin, January 22, 1899
23   Berlin, March 6, 1899
24   Berlin, April 19, 1899
25   Berlin, May 27, 1899
26   Berlin, June 3, 1899
27   Gräfenberg, August 2, 1899
28   Berlin, September 24, 1899
29   Berlin, December 17, 1899
30   Berlin, ca. January 13, 1900
31   Berlin, ca. January 22, 1900
32   Berlin, March 15, 1900
33   Berlin, March 29, 1900
34   Berlin, April 24, 1900
35   Berlin, April 30, 1900
36   Berlin, May 2, 1900
37   Berlin, ca. May 9, 1900
38   Berlin, May 25, 1900
39   Berlin, May 31, 1900
40   Berlin, June 9, 1900
41   Berlin, ca. July 3, 1900
42   Berlin, July 26, 1900

Together: 1900–1906

43   Mainz, September 21, 1900
44   Bydgoszcz, June 9, 1901
45   Rawicz, June 25, 1901
46   Berlin, January 6, 1902
47   Berlin, January 20, 1902
48   Berlin, January 28, 1902
49   Berlin, February 11, 1902
50   Berlin, February 21, 1902
51   Bydgoszcz, May 28, 1903
52   Piła, May 29, 1903
53   Glauchau, June 10, 1903

54 Hamburg, June 24, 1903
55 Dresden, September 19, 1903
56 Zwickau, September 9, 1904
57 Zwickau, September 23, 1904
58 Zwickau, October 4, 1904
59 Berlin, May 21, 1905
60 Berlin, May 26, 1905
61 Berlin, September 17, 1905
62 Berlin, September 17, 1905
63 Berlin/Jena, September 17, 1905
64 Berlin, October 10, 1905
65 Berlin, October 18, 1905
66 Berlin, October 20, 1905
67 Berlin, October 26–27, 1905
68 Berlin, November 3, 1905
69 Berlin–Friedenau, November 25, 1905
70 Berlin–Friedenau, November 27, 1905
71 Berlin–Friedenau, November 28, 1905

Unto Death: 1907-1914

72 Berlin, June 6 or 7, 1908
73 Berlin, ca. June 12, 1908?
74 Berlin, April 1909?
75 Berlin, September 1909?
76 Berlin, ca. November 15, 1909
77 Berlin, ca. November 20, 1909
78 Berlin, end of April 1910
79 Berlin, April 29, 1910
80 Berlin, ca. July 18, 1910
81 Aeschi, Switzerland, August 1 or 2, 1910
82 Aeschi, Switzerland, August 5, 1910
83 Magdeburg or Berlin, September 23, 1910
84 Berlin, ca. October 9, 1910
85 Berlin, October 11, 1910
86 Berlin, February 23, 1911

87   Berlin, March 1911?
88   Berlin, March 31, 1912
89   Berlin, beginning of April 1912
90   Berlin, July 1912
91   Berlin, August 1912
92   Berlin, beginning of October 1912
93   Berlin, May 28, 1913
94   London, December 14, 1913
95   Berlin, 1913?
96   Berlin, 1913?
97   Berlin, 1913
98   1913?
99   1913?
100 1913?
101 Berlin, beginning of April 1914
102 Berlin, June 13, 1914
103 Berlin, July 2, 1914

Index

Abramowicz, Rachela, 48, 49n
Accumulation of Capital, The,
  163, 181
Akselrod, Pavel, 48, 49n, 102,
  118n
Arbeiterin, Die, 53n
Atheneum, 15, 16n
Auer, Ignaz, 32, 36n, 37, 38,
  39, 53, 57, 117, 122, 134, 135

Basia. *See* Szpiro, Barbara
Bebel, August, 28, 32, 36n, 40,
  67, 69n, 84, 87n, 90, 103, 116,
  122, 123, 124, 136, 141, 154,
  156, 161
Berliner Tageblatt, 135, 139, 153,
  178
Bernstein, Eduard, 28, 44–45,
  49n, 53–54, 56, 58, 66, 68,
  69n, 79, 84, 96, 101
Bielecki, Jan, 15, 16n
Bolsheviks, 49n, 69n, 110–111,
  150, 151n, 174, 181, 182, 182n
Braun, Lili, 123, 124, 124n, 179
Bronstein, Lev. *See* Trotsky,
  Leon
Bruhns, Julius, 39, 41n, 42, 43,
  55
Brzezina, Karol, 9, 13n, 17

Calwer (Calver), Richard, 116,
  117n, 156
Chauvin, René, 12, 14n
Chlosta, Michał, 39n, 41n
Chrzanowska-Warska, Jadwiga
  (Jadzia), 10, 12, 14n, 19, 20,
  32, 35, 61
Communist International, 13n,
  144n
Communist Manifesto, The, 137,
  138
Cunow, Heinrich, 90, 91n, 129,
  141, 156

Das Kapital, 96, 101
Daszyński, Ignacy, 36, 36n
Defnet, Alfred, 10, 14n
Devenir Social, 62, 63, 64
Dietz, J. H. W., 90, 91n, 137,
  138n
Dobranicki, Mieczysław, 143
Donninges, Helena (Helene
  von Dönninges), 35, 36n
Dortumunder Arbeiterzeitung, 176
Dreyfus affair, 62, 66, 82, 83n
Dubreuilh, Louis, 122, 124n
Dubrowiński, Josif F.
  (Innokentii), 174
Duncker. *See* Verlag Duncker
  and Humblot

Dzierżyński, Feliks (Józef), 174,
174n, 175n, 179, 196

Eisner, Kurt, 83, 85n, 116, 120–
121, 122, 156
Engels, Friedrich, 101, 176n
Eulenberg, Albert, 47, 52
Eyth, Max, 184

Falkenhayn, Erich von, 164
Feinstein, Władysław (Witold),
143, 144
Fischer, Kuno, 48
Forrer, R., 78, 80n, 98, 100
Fröhlich, Paul, 183n
Fröhlich, Rosi, 183n
From the Battlefield, 111, 150,
151n
From the Revolutionary Era, 142
Fürstenberg-Hanecki, Jakub,
159, 159n

Ganelin, Salomon, 48, 49n
Gerisch, K. A., 134, 134n
German Communist Party,
66n, 67n, 112, 190, 191
German Social Democratic
Party (SPD), 28, 29, 36n, 38n,
49n, 67n, 79n, 85n, 91n, 110,
116–117, 117n, 118n, 124n,
132n, 134n, 147n, 155n, 161,
163, 176n, 177n, 179, 183n,
190
Gleichheit, Die, 67n, 123, 124,
144n
Goethe, Johann Wolfgang von,
71, 148–149
Goldendach-Riazanov, Dawid
B., 150, 151n
Gordon, Anna, 12, 13, 14n, 98
Gorki, Maxim, 157–158, 158n
Gradnauer, Georg, 122, 124n,
135
Grozowski (pseud. for LJ), 83n

Guesde, Jules, 3, 12, 14n
Gut, Stanisław, 39, 41n

Haenisch, Konrad, 77, 79n, 176
Harburger Volksblatt, 135
Hartman, Mieczysław (Mitek),
8, 13
Heine, Heinrich, 140, 189
Heinrich, Władysław, 8, 9, 13n,
15, 75
Helphand, Alexander Israel
(Parvus), 39, 41n, 48, 52, 56,
66, 67, 83, 84–85, 137, 150,
157–158, 158n
Herkner, Heinrich, 35, 57
Hirschfeld-Tenenbaum, Edda,
143, 144n
Hobson, John Atkinson, 79
Humblot. See Verlag Duncker
and Humblot

Ihrer, Emma, 52, 53n
Independent Social Democratic
Party, 69n
Industrial Development of Poland,
The, 19n, 28, 58, 59n, 181n
Innokentii. See Dubrowiński,
Josif
International Bureau of the
Socialist International, 182n
Introduction to Political Economy,
163
Iskra, 118n, 150, 151, 182

Jadzia. See Chrzanowska-
Warska, Jadwiga
Jaurès, Jean, 3, 62, 62n, 66
Jogiches, Emilia (sister of LJ),
2–3
Jogiches, Jakub (grandfather of
LJ), 2
Jogiches, Józef (Osip, brother of
LJ), 3, 118–119, 120
Jogiches, Pavel (brother of LJ),
3, 172, 173n

Jogiches, Samuel (father of LJ),
    2
Jogiches, Zofia (mother of LJ),
    2, 36n, 46
Józio. See Luxemburg, Józef
Junius Pamphlet, 190

Kaden, A. W., 66, 67n
Kasprzak, Marcin, 40, 42n, 133,
    147
Kautsky, Benedikt, 103n, 120
Kautsky, Karl, 28, 66n, 67, 69n,
    72, 73, 75, 78, 80, 83, 84, 85n,
    86, 87, 87n, 89, 90, 91, 96,
    101, 119, 120, 122, 123, 128,
    137, 141, 145, 146, 153, 154,
    155, 157, 161, 172, 176, 176n,
    182, 182n
Kautsky, Luise, 57n, 69n, 78,
    87, 102, 102n-103n, 120, 122,
    138, 145, 146, 153, 154, 157
Kautskyites, 179n
Kelles-Krauz, Kazimierz, 64,
    65n
Kladderadatsch, 138, 139n
Kölnische Zeitung, 61, 65
KPP. See Polish Communist
    Party
Krakus. See Stein, Henryk
Krichevsky, Boris N., 10, 11,
    13, 13n, 70, 101, 123

Lafargue, Paul, 12, 14n, 96
Lavigne, Raymond, 141, 141n
Lavrov, Piotr, 9, 13n, 14
Ledebour, Georg, 48, 49n, 66n,
    67-68, 116, 122-123, 170
Leipziger Volkszeitung, 45, 49n,
    51, 56, 65, 66, 68, 75n, 83, 96,
    105, 110, 126-132, 132n, 148,
    176, 186n
Lenin, Vladimir Ylyich, 49n,
    67n, 69n, 110-111, 112, 118n,
    150, 151n, 174n, 178, 181n,
    182, 182n

Liebknecht, Wilhelm, 28, 36n
Litvinov, M. M., 182, 182n
Löwenstein, Lina. See
    Luxemburg, Lina
Lübeck, Gustav, 27, 78, 100,
    104
Lübeck, Karol, 40
Lübeck, Olympia, 27, 152
Luxemburg, Anna (Andzia,
    sister of RL), 1, 41n, 129, 149,
    152, 184n
Luxemburg, Elias Eduard
    (father of RL), 1, 29, 59-60,
    80, 81-82, 83n, 87, 90, 99, 152
Luxemburg, Józef (Józio,
    brother of RL), 1, 39, 41n, 52,
    53, 57, 59-60, 63, 81, 137,
    152, 157
Luxemburg, Lili (sister-in-law
    of RL), 136, 137
Luxemburg, Lina (mother of
    RL), 1, 29, 81, 83n, 140, 141n,
    152
Luxemburg, Maksymilian
    (Munio, brother of RL), 1, 42,
    132, 137, 157, 158, 172, 173,
    174, 179n
Luxemburg, Mikołaj (brother of
    RL), 1, 41-42

Marchlewski, Julian, 9, 10, 13n,
    17, 92, 123, 143, 145, 152,
    186, 196
Marx, Karl, 28, 45, 66, 79, 96,
    101-102, 137, 155, 176
Mehring, Eva, 185
Mehring, Franz, 28, 66n, 67,
    68, 78, 122, 126-127, 129,
    130-133, 158, 172, 176, 185,
    186
Mendelson, Stanisław, 158
Mensheviks, 49, 118, 151, 182
"Militia and Militarism," 75
Mill, Josif, 77, 79
Mink, Paula, 12, 14n

Mitek. *See* Hartman,
  Mieczysław
Molotov, V. M., 182
Morawski, Franciszek, 37, 38n,
  44-45
Mouvement Socialiste, 84
Mozhdzhensky, Gabriel, 13,
  14n
Müller, Clara, 122
Munio. *See* Luxemburg,
  Maksymilian

"National Question and
  Autonomy, The," 163
Neue Zeit, 45, 48, 49n, 54, 86,
  91n, 96, 101, 102, 103, 110,
  121, 130, 131, 141, 176
Neufeld (RL's landlord), 128

Olszewski, Władysław, 39, 41n,
  63

Paris Commune celebration, 12,
  20
Partitioning of Poland, 195
Parvus. *See* Helphand,
  Alexander Israel
Petite République, 48, 56, 84, 123
Pieck, Wilhelm, 183n
Piłsudski, Józef, 182, 195
Platter, Julius, 48, 49n
Plekhanov, Georgii V., 2, 118n,
  182, 182n
Płochocki, L., 91, 92n
Polish Communist Party (KPP),
  196
Polish Social Democratic Party
  (PPSD), 36n
Polish Socialist Party (PPS), 17,
  36n, 38n, 65, 92n, 96, 96n,
  99, 100, 154, 158, 158n, 182,
  195, 196
Polish United Workers' Party,
  151n, 196

Polish Workers' Party, 144n,
  196
Popławski, Wojciech, 39, 41n
Potresov, Aleksander N., 119,
  121
PPS. *See* Polish Socialist Party
PPSD. *See* Polish Social
  Democratic Party
Proletariat, 195, 196

Radek, Karol (Sobelson), 170,
  171, 174, 180
Red Banner, The, 111, 142, 143n,
  144, 171, 179
Reiff, Adolf, 11, 14n, 17, 19
Raisanov. *See* Goldendach-
  Riazanov, Dawid B.
Robotnik, 195
Rodbertus-Jagetsov, Karl
  Johann, 71
Roland-Holst, Henrietta, 158,
  158n
Rosenfeld, Kurt, 186, 186n
Rote Fahn, Die, 191
Russian Revolution, 69-70, 110-
  111, 112, 174
Russian Social-Democratic
  Workers' Party, 29, 48, 49n,
  110, 118n, 162, 178n, 181n,
  182n

Sächsische Arbeiterzeitung, 28, 46,
  49n, 54, 66n, 67, 68, 83, 124n,
  129, 131, 132n, 155
Schippel, Max, 66, 67n, 72,
  75n, 129
Schönlank, Bruno, 45, 47, 49n,
  53, 55, 61-62, 65, 66, 68, 71,
  77, 83, 83n, 84, 86, 104, 105,
  128
SDKP. *See* Social Democracy of
  the Kingdom of Poland
SDKPiL. *See* Social Democracy
  of the Kingdom of Poland
  and Lithuania

Seidel, Mathilde, 39, 41, 41n, 185
Seidel, Robert, 39, 41, 41n, 63, 66, 185
Shmuilov-Claassen, Vladimir, 35, 36n, 61
Sigg, J., 149, 149n
Simplicissimus, 35, 36
Singer, Paul, 90, 116, 117n, 121, 123
Sobelson, Karol. *See* Redek, Karol
Social Democracy of the Kingdom of Poland and Lithuania (SDKPiL), xviii, 2, 3, 22, 41n, 42n, 92n, 111, 143n, 144n, 151n, 159, 159n, 162, 170n, 171n, 172n, 174n, 175n, 180, 196
Social-Democratic Review, The, 170, 170n, 171, 172
Socialist International, 3, 28, 36n, 62n, 164, 182n
"Social Reform or Revolution," 28, 76
Soyuz, 70
Sozialdemokrat, Der, 67n, 77
Sozialistische Monatshefte, 61, 63, 152
Spartakusbund, 67n, 190
SPD. *See* German Social Democratic Party
Stadthagen, Arthur, 66, 67n, 78, 104, 104n, 120, 122
Stampfer, Friedrich, 132n–133n
Stein, Henryk, 175, 175n
"Step by Step," 45, 49n, 74
Stock, Emmy, 122, 124n
Struve, Piotr B., 81, 87n, 91
Suffrage, universal, 177n
Szebs, Reinhold (Schebs), 39, 41n
Szirman, 59, 62n, 70
Szpiro, Barbara, 174, 175n

Trepov, F. (General), 2, 118
Trial, 1914, 186n
Trotsky, Leon (Lev Bronstein), 150, 151n, 174
Tych, F., 79n

Urbach, Ignacy, 62, 63n, 65, 66

Vaillant, Edouard, 3
Verlag Duncker and Humblot, 35, 36n, 40, 45, 52, 53, 56
Volkswacht, 118
Volkszeitung, 131
Vollmar, Georg von, 116, 117n
Vorwärts, 48, 49n, 65, 67n, 83, 84, 85n, 95, 99, 123, 131, 153, 155, 156, 158, 159, 172, 176, 177, 180, 186, 187n
Vossische Zeitung, 154

Walewska, Countess, 112, 157
Wallfisch, Herman, 185
Warski. *See* Warszawski-Warski, Adolf
Warszawski-Warski, Adolf, 8, 9, 10, 11, 12, 13n, 20, 32, 57, 61, 76, 121, 137, 157, 174, 178, 181
Waryński, Ludwik, 195
"What Do We Want," 150, 151
"What Next?," 142, 143, 144
Wiethölter, C. (LJ's tailor), 178, 178n
Wilhelm II, 111, 138
Winter, August, 37, 38, 38n, 40, 42, 45, 51, 58
Wojnarowska, Cezaryna Wanda, 19, 22n, 158
Wolf, Julius, 41, 42n, 57
Women and Socialism (W. Liebknecht), 36n
Workers' Cause, The, 3, 8, 9, 13, 15, 19
Workers' Journal, The, 38n, 65, 96, 99

Workers' Magazine, The, 151n, 154
World War I, 189–190
Wurm, Emanuel, 146, 147n, 158
Wurm, Mathilde, 146, 147n

Żaba. *See* Popławski, Wojciech
Zasulich, Vera, 2, 119
Zetkin, Clara, 28, 53n, 66, 67n, 92, 94, 117, 132, 136, 137, 147, 161, 178
Zetkin, Konstantin, 107n, 111, 161–162
Zévaès, Alexandre, 12, 14n